YOU'RE HIRED! CV

HOW TO WRITE A BRILLIANT CV

CORINNE MILLS

To Jonathan, Elliot and Louis
Thank you for your love and patience.

You're Hired! CV: how to write a brilliant CV

This first edition published in 2009 by Trotman Publishing, a division of Crimson Publishing Ltd., Westminster House, Kew Road, Richmond, Surrey TW9 2ND

© Trotman Publishing 2009

Author Corinne Mills

British Library Cataloguing in Publication Data
A catalogue record for this book is available from the British Library

ISBN 978 1 84455 177 4

Designed by Nicki Averill
Typeset by RefineCatch Ltd, Bungay, Suffolk
Printed and bound in Great Britain by TJ International Ltd, Padstow, Cornwall

CONTENTS

LIST OF ACTIVITIES

ABOUT THE AUTHOR

Corinne Mills is MD of Personal Career Management, one of the UK's leading and most innovative career-coaching companies, specialising in helping individuals make informed career decisions and obtain the role they want. She also works with organisations on their talent-management programmes and outplacement.

As a qualified career coach, she has worked with thousands of individuals during her 12 years in the career management field, ranging from people on million pound salaries, to those at the start of their career. Previously working in senior HR roles, she is uniquely positioned to understand both from the candidate's and the organisation's point of view, what makes a good fit.

Corinne appears regularly in the media as a spokesperson and author on career management issues. Appearances include being the career-coaching expert on the *Tonight with Trevor MacDonald* series, BBC News, the *Guardian*, Monster and frequent radio appearances. She has also written many articles and columns for newspapers and professional journals and been a guest speaker at many industry events on a range of career-management topics. She is a Member of the Chartered Institute for Personnel and Development with an MA in Human Resources and is a CIPD committee member and external adviser for their courses.

INTRODUCTION

CV writing looks like it should be easy to do. However, anyone who has tried it knows that it is not as straightforward as it seems. This is because the seemingly innocuous CV works on many different levels. On the one hand, it is a straightforward historical record of your skills, qualifications and employment history. While on the other, it is a carefully crafted business proposal that sets out the business case for why you should be invited to interview.

It is deceptively tricky.

The chances are that you are reading this book because you have realised this, either because you are writing your CV for the first time, up-dating your old one or because your existing one isn't getting you shortlisted. Whether you are a first-time job-seeker or a seasoned employee, you are also likely to be aware that the quality of your working life and the career opportunities that you can access are likely to be influenced by the effectiveness of your CV. Your CV can mean the difference between falling at the very first recruitment fence or going on to win the race.

The aim of this book is to help you create a CV that is going to get you to the interview for the job you want and position you as a front-runner for the interview finishing line.

Divided into logical sections, the book helps you gather the information you need and then build a CV which offers a meaningful and highly persuasive portrait of you as an ideal candidate.

All the chapters are clearly signposted in terms of content so that you can either read through the book from start to finish or dip into the sections of most relevance to you. Also included are activities to help you research the information you need in a more fun and accessible way. It is highly recommended that you complete these activities as you will find them invaluable as the main building blocks for your CV and as preparation for interview. You can complete them within the book or copy them onto paper or your computer. Keep them handy because you will need them often.

The great thing about your investment in this book and the time and energy you spend on working through it, is that there is a direct return. A CV that works is time efficient, can increase your earning potential and job satisfaction, and improves your employability and choices for the future. Well worth it!

Happy job-hunting!
Corinne Mills
www.personalcareermanagement.com

RESEARCHING YOU

Talking to strangers?

Before any employer will take you on, they will want to know about you in detail. Part 1 of this book is going to help you prepare the factual information that you need to present in your CV, as well as identifying the skills, abilities and personal qualities that will get you shortlisted.

There are various activities included within this section which will help you with this research. You can use the forms at the end of the chapters to record this information or create a similar template on your computer, which you can then copy to your new CV document. This research will also be helpful when it comes to prepare for interview. However you decide to compile this information, by the end of Part 1, you will have completed the first, key building block in assembling your CV.

1 GATHERING THE FACTS

At its most simple level, your CV is a historical record of who you are, what you have done and your contact details. The first step therefore in writing a new CV, or even revising an old one, is to ensure that the facts are complete, accurate and appropriate. This chapter is going to help you gather together and check that you have all of the factual information about yourself that is needed.

This chapter will help you:

■ identify the essential information you need to include on your CV

■ decide which optional information you want to include

■ identify information that should definitely be left out

■ collect the information you need for easy reference.

Fact not fiction

Every CV should include the following factual information:

- name and full contact details
- details of your career history
- educational record
- any professional qualifications and/or professional memberships
- relevant skills and knowledge
- relevant training and development.

Although this seems very straightforward, getting it wrong, as candidates frequently do, can have serious implications. Factual information that has been supplied by a candidate and which is found to be false, may exclude you from any other applications to that organisation. Even if it is discovered *after* you have been employed for some time, the employer could still legitimately dismiss you for gross misconduct.

So let's go through each of the above items in the list in turn to make sure there are no omissions or gaffes.

Contact details

Name
Decide the name you want to be referred to and stick to this throughout. In your private life people may call you something slightly different, e.g. Robert or Bob, but try to ensure that you refer to yourself in a consistent way to avoid any confusion. If you have a fairly common name, e.g. John Brown, then you may wish to add an initial to differentiate yourself.

Telephone contact number(s)
It is now acceptable just to quote your mobile number as your preferred point of contact. However, if you do this, ensure that you keep your mobile charged, topped up with credits if you are on a 'pay as you go' plan, and check for voicemails regularly.

The voicemail may be the first time that a potential employer hears your voice, so make sure the message is suitably clear and professional. Jokey voicemails may be fun but are not going to set the right tone for you as a serious candidate. Employers who are unable to contact you immediately or leave a message will be unlikely to ring back. Their view will be that if you could not organise a working voicemail, you are unlikely to have the professional approach that they are looking for.

If you provide your home number, then ensure that anyone who could pick up the phone is ready and equipped to take messages. They need to note down the person's name, company, contact number and pass it on to you quickly. Opportunities do get missed because messages are not passed on promptly or properly, so make sure that you leave clear instructions.

If you are currently working, do not give your current work telephone number as a contact number unless your manager is aware that you are looking for a job and is supportive. It's too risky.

Email address

Try using a personal email address for your job-searching activities rather than a current work email address (if you have one). Many companies now have an internet and email policy that warns employees that their facilities are for company business only and they will take action over inappropriate use.

It's not a great idea to risk disciplinary proceedings when you are looking for your next job, so just play it safe and set up your own personal email facility. You can set one up quickly and easily using services such as Gmail, Hotmail or Yahoo. The advantages of these email addresses are that they are free, confidential and you can access them from anywhere that has internet access. You can also set up this email address specifically for job-searching and close it down at a later date if you have no need for it, or if it becomes a magnet for spam.

Make sure that your email address is suitably professional. Your surname with initials or numbers usually works best. However, avoid using 'O' or 'I' unless they are part of a recognisable word. This is because it can be difficult for email senders to distinguish between the letters 'O' or 'I' and the numbers 'zero' or 'one', respectively. For example, Olivia222@hotmail.com is clear whereas OliviaIII@hotmail.com makes it difficult to see whether the 'I' is a capital 'i' or a lower case 'L' or the number '1'.

Be aware also that email addresses you currently use, perhaps with your friends, may be inappropriate for prospective employers, e.g. jonathan@sexanddrugs.com. This will certainly create a strong impression, but just not necessarily the right one.

> I'm just under average height and so called myself 'little Alex' in my email address. However, it wasn't until it was pointed out to me, that I realised that this could be creating a false impression and was potentially very sensitive. I changed my email address.
>
> *Alex Care*
> *Project Manager*
> *Real-life Projects*

Many couples share an email, e.g. simonandliz@email.com especially when it is a shared home computer account. However, this is now considered old fashioned and rather twee. Employers want to write to you, not your family. Obtain your own email address.

Career background

Employers will want to know details of your work experience, educational background, professional memberships, etc. Each aspect is discussed below and you can use the forms in Activity 1 on page 22 at the end of this chapter to record all of your relevant information.

Career history

- **Previous employers:** list all of your previous employers with some additional information about their size, turnover, key products or services. You can use this information later to draw attention to any similarities between your previous organisation and the one you are applying to, e.g. similar turnover, products, multi-site locations.
- **Dates of employment:** these are essential to get right. You can enter the dates as month to month or even year to year if you want to cover gaps of a few months. However, these must be 100% accurate. Employers will check with previous employers the dates that you worked for them and your P45 will clearly state your date of leaving. Some companies even hire external specialists to double-check information on previous employment supplied by candidates. Any doubt about the date you have given them may lead them to question whether the other information you have supplied is accurate. Don't be caught out by some casual error that could cost you the job offer.
- **Key duties and responsibilities:** for each role, include some brief bullet points about the key duties you performed. Employers want to know the scope and size of your role so try to quantify this, for example:
  - What staff responsibilities did you have? How many staff did you recruit, train, appraise, manage, etc.?
  - Did you manage a budget and if so for how much?
  - Who were your customers? How big were their accounts?
  - How often did you need to write reports, correspondence, give presentations, etc.
  - Did you have any national, international or cross-organisational responsibilities?
  - Did you help bring business into the company, and if so, what did you do and how much was it worth?

Vocational qualifications and/or professional memberships

List any qualifications you have achieved which are industry related or recognised by professional associations. These could include certificates, diplomas, BTECs, NVQs, degrees or post-graduate training, e.g. certificate in counselling, diploma in social care, post-graduate degree in education.

If you are already working in a specific field, you should also list any memberships of compulsory and voluntary organisations, e.g. the General Medical Council, the Chartered Institute of Public Relations. Such organisations often require members to work to certain standards and ethics and take professional exams. Listing your memberships and membership grade if appropriate (e.g. Fellow) will demonstrate your professional credibility and commitment to standards.

Training and development

Note any training or development that you have undertaken. This could include any of the following:

- in-house courses, such as customer service
- external courses, such as PRINCE2
- e-Learning packages, such as MCSE Microsoft engineer packages
- ongoing courses, such as Open University study
- extensive reading on particular subjects such as diversity issues
- being on the fast-track 'talent pool' at work
- workplace or career coaching
- voluntary work training, such as learning listening skills as a Samaritan
- distance-learning courses
- attendance at conferences and seminars
- participation in action-learning groups
- mentoring or being mentored
- secondment opportunities
- health and safety, first aid, risk assessment.

Make a note of any courses you are currently undertaking and their estimated completion date. Employers like to see that you are continually learning and updating your skills.

University or college education

Write down details of any degree or college courses for which you have studied. Note the grade achieved, the dates of study and the name of the institution. Where you have more than one degree, list them all, with the most recent or the most relevant first.

Secondary school education

Write down all of the qualifications you attained at school and your dates of study and exam achievements. Normally, your CV should include information on your secondary school achievements only if you have less than five years' job experience and/or do not have a higher academic qualification such as a degree.

However, you could include your secondary school education if you had excellent A level results but disappointing university grades. If you do this, then be prepared to talk at interview about why your degree results were poor by comparison. The fact that you were too busy partying is not going to impress the employer. However, they may well have sympathy for other mitigating circumstances.

If you are a first-time job-seeker, you should also make a note of other school activities in which you were involved to show off your capabilities. Examples include:

- any awards or prizes gained
- any relevant projects undertaken, e.g. participation in school business challenge
- any sports achievements
- any voluntary work undertaken
- being head girl or boy
- being a school council member or holding another position of responsibility
- organising events, e.g. summer fairs.

Knowledge

Write down the specific areas of knowledge you have of a subject, including specific industry or sector knowledge, for example:

- advising managers on employment law
- change management within the mobile telecommunications sector
- direct marketing for charities
- financial databases used for budget management and forecasting
- maintenance of home burglar alarm systems
- merchandising for fashion stores
- software programing languages for data warehousing
- understanding the workings of the National Health Service (NHS) including recent government initiatives.

MAKING THE GRADE!

If you've ever been tempted to 'improve' your grades on your CV...

- Employers will often check your academic record and may ask you to bring in your certificates.

- If you lie and are found out, then any job offer is likely to be withdrawn.

- You can be dismissed at any time if you are found to have lied at the recruitment stage. High-profile examples include Patrick Imbardelli, who in 2007 was about to be promoted to the main board of Inter-Continental Hotels when it was discovered that he had lied about his academic qualifications. He was fired in disgrace from his £300,000 job by his long-standing employer. Imagine trying to get a reference after that!

- Academic qualifications are most important at the start of your career, but become less important the more experienced you become.

- Many successful people have risen to the top despite poor academic qualifications, for example Richard Branson and Bill Gates.

- There are lots of opportunities to continue your education and training while you work, including Open University and distance-learning programmes. There are even schemes to accredit your work experience and translate this into academic points.

- If you have relevant experience, showing that you are working towards a qualification even if you have not achieved it yet, it can sometimes be sufficient to get you on the shortlist for a job where this is a requirement.

Information technology (IT) packages

These are such an essential skill that it is worth noting all IT capabilities and your level of ability.

Publications/research/conferences/working groups

This is usually more relevant for academic staff, consultants or anyone who is seeking to position themselves as an acknowledged authority in a particular area. How do you show you are a leading industry expert? One way to demonstrate your prowess is by listing research papers and publications, consultancy projects, media activities or conferences you have attended as a speaker. Write down any industry- or subject-related working groups in which you participate. Include any instances where your advice has been sought outside your current organisation.

Hobbies/interests

Write down all your hobbies and interests. It is not strictly necessary to include this on your CV, but it sometimes has advantages. If you are going for a job as a sales assistant in a bookshop, it makes sense to put down reading as one of your hobbies. Interesting hobbies can also enliven an otherwise conventional CV. A secretary who is a champion water-skier – fantastic! Sports and physical recreation activities are useful to include because they indicate you are fit and healthy. This is particularly relevant if you are more mature in years and want to demonstrate that you have bundles of energy. Listing only solitary activities such as bird-watching, stamp-collecting and playing video games may lead the recruiter to wonder how sociable you are.

Gaming and online networking are popular and fast-growing social activities. However, be aware that if you mention social networking websites, employers may well be prompted to investigate your online profile on sites such as Facebook. Be careful what you publish on the web as it may be seen by a prospective, or even your current, employer.

Most importantly, if you decide to include a hobby on your CV, then make sure it is genuine and that you can talk about it at the interview. Many a promising candidate has scuppered their chances by writing about their theatre-going or mountain-climbing activities, only for it to emerge at interview that they can't remember the last play they saw and the mountain-climbing was a one-off as a result of taking a wrong turning.

Voluntary work

Think of all the voluntary activities you have been involved in over the past few years. This could include fundraising, helping out at your local school, running a local football team or sitting on a local committee.

Employers are often interested in socially responsible activities. They indicate energy and community spirit, the kind of behaviours they want you to employ for their organisation.

They can also demonstrate that you have capabilities over and above your paid work experience. Taking a strategic role on an advisory committee, using advanced interpersonal skills in working

> If you want to claim 'industry expert' status then you need to demonstrate that your knowledge is highly regarded by others apart from your immediate employer. Articles, original research, participating in relevant committees can help to raise your industry profile and look impressive on your CV.
>
> *Delia Goldring*
> *Visiting Professor,*
> *Middlesex University*
> *Business School*

> Be wary as to what you put as your interests. When I see 'reading and socialising' as someone's only interests, I start to worry. Socialising is a basic human requirement so you might as well put 'eating, breathing, going to bathroom in spare time'.
>
> *Peter Lockhart*
> *Executive Recruiter,*
> *Ward Simpson*

VOLUNTARY WORK IS A GREAT WAY TO ENHANCE YOUR CV

- In the UK, there are currently 11.6 million people volunteering at least once a month and 17.9 million people at least once a year.

- Employers often want you to have experience – and volunteering can be a way of getting this experience. Most employers will see voluntary work as valuable as any paid job – the important thing is to sell your knowledge, skills and experience gained. Voluntary roles can cover anything from fundraising to befriending an isolated, vulnerable person or press work in a major national charity.

- As well as developing your work experience and building your confidence, you will learn new skills and you might be offered the chance to study or train for a qualification.

- For career changers, volunteering can provide the chance to sample a new role, and a way into working in a completely new field – including paid opportunities within the charity sector itself.

Katie Hall
UK Workforce Hub, National Council for
Voluntary Organisations

with vulnerable people, or using financial skills as treasurer are good examples of ways in which you can help bridge perceived gaps in your paid work experience when applying for a new role. It helps to demonstrate to an employer that you are serious about your next career move because you have invested unpaid time and energy to progress your career in this direction.

If you aren't working currently and have a gap since your last job, enrolling yourself to do some voluntary work at least a few hours a week will be enormously beneficial. It will give you an answer to the interview question 'So what have you been doing since your last job?', and you will also develop skills and network contacts.

Additional information

Think about whether there is any other information about you which may be of use to an employer. These could include having:

- a driving licence
- dual citizenship
- language skills

■ rights to work in the UK if you are a non-European Union (EU) citizen
■ other roles undertaken, e.g. magistrate, non-executive director.

Referees

Identify two individuals who will be happy to act as a referee for you. Ideally they should be your current and past managers. If this is problematic, then you could use someone equivalent in seniority within the same organisation or someone with whom you had a key business relationship, for example a customer whose account you managed. If you are a first-time job-seeker, you can ask your course tutor to provide a reference.

I had a candidate's referee on the phone who was very reluctant to give a reference for the applicant (who had specifically given me his name and number). When I asked whether the candidate had performed his duties to the company's satisfaction his reply was:

'I'm sure there was nothing wrong with his work, but since I found out he's been sleeping with my wife I'm finding it difficult to say anything nice about him.'

Michelle Foreman
Human Resources
Manager

Always check with your referees that they are happy for their details to be forwarded to prospective employers. Do not assume that they will be happy to do so. The last thing you want is a referee who is unhappy with you because you haven't extended them the courtesy of asking them.

Although you need to have your referee's details handy, do not include them on your CV. The only exception to this is if they are extremely well known in their field and likely to be well regarded by the recruiter. Then definitely show off your connections.

Why is it important to retain control of your referees? If your current manager is a referee and they are not yet aware that you are looking for a new role, you need to make sure that they are going to offer you the job before you hand over your manager's contact details. It also gives you an opportunity to brief your referees on the job you are applying for and what you think the prospective employer would like to know about you. You can then remind them of all the wonderful things you did for them that demonstrate how you meet the employer's requirements. This is especially helpful if you are going for a different type of job and need your referee to be 'on message' regarding your transferable skills.

If the employer says they want referees at the start of the recruitment process, say that you are happy to supply references after your interview. Most job offers are made subject to references so it's not usually a problem, and handling it this way means that you can use your referees to best advantage.

Optional information to include on your CV

Date of birth

Since the introduction of age discrimination legislation in the UK in 2006, it has been unlawful to discriminate against candidates because of their age. Employers must consider your suitability in terms of your skills and experience, not how young or how old you are. Some companies will actually ask you to remove your age from your CV to support their equal opportunities policies.

However, it is usually possible to determine roughly a person's age because of the dates of their qualifications and experience. So omitting your date of birth is not a foolproof method of avoiding direct or indirect age discrimination.

If you are concerned that your age may work against you, leave out your date of birth. You may also choose to omit any work experience or background over 20 years old unless directly relevant to the role in question. If you are relatively early in your career, putting your date of birth can help to quickly put into context why you haven't got much work experience yet.

Nationality/work status

The UK has strict guidelines regarding the employment of workers from outside the EU, and employers face legal prosecution if they employ someone without the right to work in the UK.

EU citizens have full rights to work in the UK, so if your background and experience are predominantly from outside the EU, it is helpful to state your citizenship/work status. This will help the employer know whether you are immediately available to work. The eligibility arrangements are subject to change, which means that international candidates need to proactively check their permissions to work.

Information you should definitely leave out of your CV

Marital/family status

There is no requirement to include your marital status, number of children or other dependants and little value in doing so. What were accepted stereotypes 15–20 years ago, no longer apply. Nowadays, married status is seen as no more an indicator of stability than single status guarantees that the individual is free of personal responsibilities.

Religion, sexuality, political affiliations

Do not include religion, sexuality or political affiliations in your CV. The only exception to this would be where these were specifically relevant to the role in question, for example working with a particular group or community. In this event, it would be more appropriate to include it in a covering letter as part of your supporting evidence about why you are a suitable candidate.

Religion is a sensitive issue within the workplace. Employers are legally required to abide by anti-discrimination legislation, but as a candidate it is sometimes difficult to know if or when during the recruitment process it is appropriate to raise religious requirements.

If the religious arrangements you require are likely to be fairly straightforward, for example taking annual leave during religious festivals, you may wish to raise it either at the interview or when the job has been offered. However, if the terms on which you are available to work are less easy to arrange and/or could impact on the company's business operations, it may be easier to raise it earlier in the recruitment process either in a covering letter or in a telephone conversation.

Disabilities

It can sometimes be a difficult decision whether to disclose a disability. However, if a disability is likely to be apparent to the employer, or you will need some additional arrangement at the interview or once you start work, it may be advisable to disclose it. This will of course depend on each individual circumstance.

As with any sensitive information, it is recommended that if you wish to raise this, do so by covering letter, telephone or in person, where you can explain in more detail. Do not include disability details on your CV where space is more limited as it should retain a clear focus on your skills and capabilities.

Ill-health

Do not refer in your CV to periods of ill-health, especially if it is unlikely to have any effect on your capacity to work in the future. However, if the illness does in some way impact on your work, then like a disability issue you may want to raise it, but it is best to do this in a covering letter. You may be required to undertake an occupational health assessment at which you will need to declare your health record. However, you may also have rights under the Disability Discrimination Act for certain conditions.

The Equality and Human Rights Commission (www.equalityhumanrights.com) has more information and guidance for people affected by disability or health issues.

Reasons for leaving

Some application forms ask for reasons for leaving an organisation. This is not required on a CV – so don't volunteer it. The recruiter is considering hiring you so they don't want to be reminded by your CV of all the times you left an organisation.

Criticisms and conflicts

Undoubtedly there will have been jobs you enjoyed more than others and some which were not enjoyable at all. You may have been made redundant, had a difficult relationship with a manager or colleague, or simply been bored by the job.

Regardless of any negative associations with previous employers, it is essential that you make no direct or implicit criticisms on your CV. Employers want to hire candidates who have had good and positive relationships with previous employers. So make sure that your CV does not contain any references or even hints of disciplinary proceedings, grievances, tribunals, complaints, bullying, harassment, personality clashes, etc. Any references to these, no matter how justified you are, will be likely to arouse suspicion by a recruiter that perhaps you could be the cause of the conflict. Speak only well of past employers.

Criminal convictions

Some, but not all organisations will ask their potential employees if they have any criminal convictions. The Rehabilitation of Offenders Act means that individuals do not usually need to disclose any convictions to an employer if their conviction is 'spent'. A conviction becomes spent when a stipulated amount of time has elapsed since the offence was committed. Prison sentences of over 2.5 years and certain offences never become spent.

If your conviction is spent and an employer asks you to disclose whether you have a criminal record then you are legally entitled to say no. It may be easier to explain any career gaps by saying that you were undertaking a training course or voluntary work or some other reason that you can part justify.

However, certain organisations are exempt from the Rehabilitation of Offenders Act, including those whose work involves contact with children or other vulnerable people, for example the NHS. These organisations will normally insist on a CRB (Criminal Record Bureau) check. For these organisations, all convictions must be declared including those deemed to be spent. So, criminal convictions need to be disclosed when:

A CV should be a positive reflection of your skills and experience, so if you have to disclose your criminal record, it is best to do this separately. You should remember that if you are not asked about your criminal record, you do not need to volunteer the information on your CV. We suggest writing a brief letter of disclosure to go with your CV or application form, so that you can give a full explanation of your criminal record and reassurance that you are still a great candidate for the job.

If you have an employment gap on your CV because of a criminal record, you could say 'not in employment' or 'unavailable to work due to personal circumstances'. You can then explain this further in a covering letter if it is necessary to disclose your criminal record, or at interview if you are questioned about it.

Ruth Parker
Helpline Manager,
NACRO

- the employer specifically asks you whether you have a criminal record and your conviction is not spent
- you have a spent conviction but the organisation is exempt from the Rehabilitation of Offenders Act.

You may also decide to disclose any conviction voluntarily if you feel this is appropriate. Clearly, disclosure needs to be handled sensitively and the best place to do this is definitely not on your CV. If you are making an initial application to an organisation you know is exempt from the Rehabilitation of Offenders Act, you can include this in a covering letter. However, if the question is asked after the interview, then this is best handled in person, either by telephone call or a meeting if appropriate.

NACRO (www.nacro.org.uk) has lots of excellent information on job-searching for ex-offenders, including full details on when convictions become spent, etc. Their freephone service on 0800 0181 259 offers advice and information on all aspects of employment, benefits, etc.

Caring responsibilities

If you have caring responsibilities then presumably you will only be applying for jobs that complement these. There is therefore no need to separately state that you have these responsibilities on your CV. If you do, then it cannot help but subconsciously raise a query in the employer's mind about your non-work commitments and availability. There is legislation in place to help employees who need time off for dependants and most organisations have some flexibility or policy about this, so there is no value in raising this as a potential issue when it is unlikely to be one.

However, if your caring responsibilities are likely to affect your ability to work the hours required, you will need to raise this. Again, this is best done in a covering letter or by telephone conversation in the first instance rather than via your CV.

TABLE 1: PERSONAL INFORMATION CHECKLIST FOR YOUR CV

	Include	Do not include	Optional
Name	✓		
Address	✓		
Telephone contact	✓ Mobile and/or home	Work telephone number	
Personal email address	✓	Work email address	
Nationality/rights to work in UK	✓ If non-EU background		
Career history	✓		
University/college education	✓		
Secondary school	✓ Only if less than 5 years' work experience		
Professional memberships	✓		
Knowledge	✓		
Training and development	✓ If relevant		
Publications, research, working groups	✓		
Voluntary work	✓		
Additional information			✓ If directly relevant
Hobbies and interests			✓
Date of birth		✓ Unless have less than 5 years' work experience	
Religion		✓	
Referees		✓	
Marital status		✓	
Sexuality		✓	
No. of children		✓	
Political affiliations		✓	
Reasons for leaving		✓	
Any conflicts with employer, colleagues, etc.		✓	
Disabilities		✓ Include in covering letter if affects ability to work	
Ill-health		✓ Include in covering letter if affects ability to work	
Criminal convictions		✓ If required to disclose these then do so in covering letter or in person, but not on CV	

INFORMATION GATHERING

Use Forms 1 and 2 to capture all the essential information given in this chapter. Alternatively you can re-create them on your computer and use them later when it comes to writing your CV or completing online applications.

FORM 1: CAREER HISTORY

Name of company and location	Company information, e.g. size, turnover, products, customers	Dates worked (m/m or y/y)	Key duties and responsibilities (no. of staff managed, budget size, projects)

FORM 2: PROFESSIONAL/VOCATIONAL QUALIFICATIONS, E.G. CIMA, NVQS

Qualification	Grade	Year achieved	Institution

Training and development, e.g. any formal or informal learning activities

Membership of professional associations (membership status)

University, college education
- University/college:
- Years attended:
- Qualification:
- Grade:
- Other achievements:
- Positions of responsibility held:

- University/college:
- Years attended:
- Qualification:
- Grade:
- Other achievements:
- Positions of responsibility held:

Secondary school(s)
- Name of school:
- Years attended:
- Qualifications achieved with grades:
- Additional information:
- Other achievements:
- Positions of responsibility held:

- Name of school:
- Years attended:
- Qualifications achieved with grades:

- Additional information:
- Other achievements:
- Positions of responsibility held:

Key knowledge (technical and sector)

IT packages

Publications/research/articles/media activities/conference speaking

Hobbies/interests

Voluntary work

Additional information, e.g. clean driving licence, achievements outside work

Referees

- Name:
- Relationship to you:
- Tel:
- Correspondence address:

- Name:
- Relationship to you:
- Tel:
- Correspondence address:

IN A NUTSHELL

This chapter has focused on ensuring that the factual information that you should include in your CV is complete, correct and appropriate. Remember to:

- make sure all the information on your CV is accurate
- ensure all of your contact details are fully functioning and business-like
- make sure that sensitive issues such as disability, criminal convictions, etc. are dealt with separately from the CV
- keep all your factual information easily accessible because you will be referring to it frequently.

2 PROVE YOURSELF

You may know that you are the best person for the job. You may feel 100% confident that your prospective employer will never find anyone as skilled as you to do the job. However, the employer doesn't know that. You have to prove it to them! This chapter looks at how you can give the employer the evidence they need that you have the skills they are looking for.

This chapter will help you:

- understand competencies and how they are used by employers

- collect the evidence to help prove your key skills and competencies

- discover the other ways that employers can test your aptitude and ability.

Are you competent?

The words 'competences' or 'competencies' are used frequently and often interchangeably throughout the recruitment process. They are also used in training and development and for promotion purposes, so it's helpful to know what these refer to and how they are used.

NB. In this book I will refer to competencies, but please be aware that these are the same as (or similar to) competences.

Most popular organisational competency terms

- ■ Communication skills
- ■ People management
- ■ Team skills
- ■ Customer service skills
- ■ Results orientation
- ■ Problem-solving.

Survey by Chartered Institute of Personnel and Development (2007)

Competencies refer to behaviours that an organisation feels are required for effective performance in a particular role. They encompass not only the individual's technical skills, knowledge and abilities, but also the way in which these are applied in practice.

The ways in which employers will assess whether you have the competencies they are looking for are by:

- ■ seeing if you can provide good examples of when you have demonstrated these competencies
- ■ observing you perform tasks or activities designed to test those competencies, e.g. at interview, assessment centre or online
- ■ giving you case studies or theoretical examples and asking you to outline your approach to the challenge set.

Unless you provide good examples in your CV giving evidence of your abilities, you are not going to get the chance to prove it to them at interview.

Which of the following two statements do you think is the more credible and why?

- I am good at handling conflict.
- My work in customer services helping clients who on occasion could be aggressive, means that I am highly experienced and able to handle conflict should it arise.

The second sentence seems much more credible because it supplies background and context. This is the key to providing the proof that an employer is looking for in your CV. If you can supply detail regarding when you have demonstrated a particular skill, the recruiter is much more likely to believe you.

At the end of this chapter, you will conduct a full self-assessment of your skills. It is likely to surface some obvious skills that you know you have, as well as ones that you might have forgotten or simply taken for granted.

Aptitude testing

Some roles require a high level of innate ability as a pre-condition for consideration as a candidate. An example is spatial awareness for a pilot. For these roles, the employer may use aptitude or ability tests to ascertain whether you have the abilities they require. These commonly are questions with a right or wrong answer.

Employers may also set practical tasks or simulations, for example a typing test or a mock sales presentation, to assess your abilities. These tests may be positioned at the start of the recruitment process so you complete these at the same time as sending in your CV. They may also accompany the interview process. Make sure you are confident that you can achieve in a test any claims you make about your abilities in your CV.

You can proactively test yourself in some key areas such as verbal reasoning by visiting some of the psychometric testing websites listed below. They feature lots of good advice and many have free practice tests for candidates to try, so you can conduct your own self-assessment. If you are considering paying for a test, it is highly recommended that before paying any money for a psychometric test you should read the guidance at the British Psychological Centre website (www.psychtesting.org.uk).

Ability tests are a measure of maximum performance. They are designed to measure the extent to which candidates are able to perform specific aspects of a particular role, for example verbal or numerical reasoning.

Howard Grosvenor
Managing Consultant, SHL

- www.shl.com: includes lots of excellent advice and free practice aptitude tests from one of the UK's largest test publishers.
- www.morrisby.com: examples of ability tests found in the Morrisby Profile tests.
- www.gmac.com: the Graduate Management Admission Council provides advice and tests for graduates applying for MBA courses.
- www.ets.org: the Educational Testing Service gives advice and access to practice questions for Graduate Management Admissions Test (GMAT), Graduate Records Examinations (GRE) and the Test of English as a Foreign Language (TOEFL).
- www.savilleconsulting.com: Saville Consulting provides aptitude preparation guides and advice.
- www.learndirect.co.uk: Learn Direct offers some aptitude tests free and will signpost you to other providers where you may access low-cost aptitude assessments.

ACTIVITY 2

IDENTIFYING YOUR SKILLS

Once you have completed this activity, remember to keep this information ready to hand because you are going to need to refer to it when it comes to writing your CV and preparing for interview.

1. The skills list given here isn't an exhaustive list but is designed as a useful prompt. Use a coloured pen to highlight which, in your opinion, are your BEST skills.

2. Write down any other skills which you have, which are not on the list.

Skills list

adapting	certifying	controlling	diagnosing
administering	chairing	coordinating	diplomacy
advising	classifying	coping	directing
analysing	coaching	counselling	displaying
anticipating	collaborating	creating	disproving
appraising	collating	cultivating	dissecting
articulating	communicating	customer service	disseminating
assembling	(telephone)	decision-making	documenting
assessing	communicating	delegating	drafting
auditing	(face-to-face)	demonstrating	drawing
briefing	computing	designing	driving
budgeting	conceptualising	detailing	editing
building	constructing	detecting	educating
calculating	consulting	developing	empathising

empowering	installing	ordering	restoring
enforcing	interpreting	organising	risk assessment
estimating	interviewing	painting	scheduling
evaluating	inventing	persuading	selling
examining	investigating	piloting	setting objectives
experimenting	judging	pioneering	simplifying
explaining	launching	planning	sorting
facilitating	leading	precision	structuring
filing	learning quickly	presenting	summarising
finalising	lecturing	prioritising	supervising
financing	liaising	problem-solving	systematising
fixing	lifting	procuring	teaching
forecasting	listening	promoting	team building
generating ideas	making	proof-reading	testing
growing plants	presentations	public speaking	time-management
guiding	managing	publicising	training
handling conflict	managing people	purchasing	trouble-shooting
helping	marketing	quantifying	using tools
illustrating	measuring	raising animals	versatility
implementing	mediating	reconciling	visualising
improving	memorising	recording	winning
improvising	mentoring	recruiting	working to deadlines
influencing	modelling	rehabilitating	working under
informing	moderating	relationship building	pressure
initiating	motivating	repairing	writing
innovating	negotiating	report writing	
inspecting	networking	representing	
inspiring	operating	researching	

PROVING YOUR SKILLS

1. Ask the opinion of someone whose opinion you trust to run through this with you. Often they will be able to remind you of examples that you have forgotten.

2. Write down at least 3 examples of how and when you used each one of the skills you have highlighted in Form 3. These may be skills you use every day or more occasionally.

FORM 3	
Your key skills	**Examples of when you have used these skills**

IN A NUTSHELL

In order to write your CV you need to have a clear, objective view of the skills and competencies you are offering an employer. This chapter has helped you:

■ identify your key skills
■ provide evidence to prove these abilities, which you can use in your CV and in your interview
■ understand that employers may also set ability tests so any claims you make on your CV regarding your abilities must be realistic.

3 HIGHLIGHTING YOUR ACHIEVEMENTS

Chapter 2 was about proving your skills and abilities to the employer. Using achievement statements in your CV is a way to show that you can use those skills, not just for their own sake, but to deliver meaningful results for the organisation. It shows employers they are likely to get a return on their investment if they hire you.

This chapter will help you:

■ understand why employers like achievements on CVs

■ identify the achievements you have made

■ write achievement statements for your CV

■ record your achievements in an easily usable form.

Value added: why employers like achievers

Many candidates write their CVs like a job description. They faithfully list the duties they performed and their responsibilities. However, they fail to show the positive impact of their work on the team or organisation as a whole.

The whole point of employing someone is that they can make a contribution to the organisation. Employers are interested in employing staff who can:

- solve a problem for them
- increase profits
- reduce costs
- sell more
- improve efficiency
- raise quality
- generate ideas
- enhance customer satisfaction.

If the employer can see that the salary they will be paying you will be more than offset by your contribution to organisational efficiency and profits, then it makes the hiring decision easier for them.

Candidates who include achievements in their CV are much more likely to be seen as dynamic, business-aware, high performers and to be viewed as a potential asset rather than a cost.

Julia Gardner

Career Coach

Including your achievements in your CV helps to present you as a person who:

- does over and above what is required in the role
- can see the relationship between their individual effort and the bigger organisational picture
- focuses on results
- likes a challenge
- gets things done.

Dutiful or high achiever?

If you are not convinced whether achievement statements make much difference on a CV, then compare the duty and achievement statements in Table 2 to see which you think are most attractive to any employer.

TABLE 2: DUTY VERSUS ACHIEVEMENT

Statements indicating 'duty'	Statements indicating 'achievement'
Responsible for inducting new staff	Inducted over 20 new staff in departmental procedures to ensure consistency of approach and high-quality customer service
Introduced mentoring scheme	Introduced mentoring scheme to over 30 new staff per year, which improved staff retention and enabled new employees to quickly become effective in their new role
Trained staff in Excel	Trained 50 staff in Excel, which increased the capabilities of staff and their time efficiency in producing reports
Purchased new factory equipment	Researched and purchased new factory equipment, which led to a 30% increase in packaging efficiency
Responsibilities include credit control	Since taking over the credit control function over 95% of long-standing debts have been recovered, some of which had been owing for more than 2 years
Responsible for pool maintenance	Reduced leakages by changing sealant, which meant existing liner could be repaired rather than replaced, saving over £5,000 in materials and staff costs

The achievement statements above reinforce the impression of the candidate as someone who understands and does their best to support the wider business needs of an organisation rather than an employee who is a 'jobsworth' doing the bare minimum.

So what have you achieved?

No matter what roles you have been working in or how long your career has been, there will be things that you have achieved and which you can use on your CV to create that positive impression. However, this is one of those activities where it is not always easy to be objective about yourself and realise the impact that you have made. So to help you, the following prompts have been designed to get you thinking about your achievements.

IDENTIFYING YOUR ACHIEVEMENTS

Think about the following questions and record your answers in Form 4 at the end of this activity.

For each role in which you have worked, aim to think of at least three to five achievements that you can include as a bullet point in your CV. You may find it helpful to reflect on the following questions.

- What positive feedback have you received at work and why?

- Have you received any awards, commendations or special mentions?

- What personal targets have you achieved?

- How have you contributed to team or organisational targets?

- What did you do that saved money, time, and resources for the organisation?

- What did you do that directly or indirectly increased profits, customers or sales?

- How did you improve the quality or efficiency in your own work or that of others?

- What did you do to improve customer service for both internal and external customers?

- What challenges or problems have you faced that you were able to overcome?

- What have you helped to change and what has been the impact?

- What ideas have you generated and what was the result?

Achievements should be predominantly work related but you can also include non-work activities that are either relevant to the type of role sought or reflect well on you in other ways.

If your role is an outcome-related one, for example sales and marketing, then your CV needs to focus heavily on results in terms of increased sales, market share, value of contracts won, etc. Try wherever possible to use numbers, percentages, size, pounds and pence, or hours to describe the results, making an estimate if the final amount is not clear-cut.

Complete the following form to help you capture the information you need.

FORM 4: YOUR ACHIEVEMENTS		
Problem, challenge, opportunity?	**How you tackled it?**	**Impact/benefits**

Writing your achievement statements

Now you need to think about how you are going to write this information in a way that you can use on your CV. Here are some guidelines to help you.

■ Try to use these formulas to help you write those statements:

Beneficial result   +   what you did that made this happen

Example: Saved management time and improved customer experience [beneficial result] by introducing an effective complaints escalation procedure [what you did].

or

What you did   +   beneficial result

Example: Introduced complaints escalation procedure [what you did] which saved management time and improved customer experience [beneficial result].

Employers invest much time and money in recruiting new staff, so they are understandably keen to get a return on that investment. They want staff who can not only do the job, but are also motivated and get on with the other people they are working with. Most of us have had experience of working with someone who is disruptive, lazy or even dishonest, and know the negative impact they can have. Employers are right to be cautious about whom they let into their organisation. If you can reassure them on your CV that you are an asset, not a liability, then you can create a competitive advantage over other candidates.

THE THREE SHORTLIST QUESTIONS

- Can you do the job?
- Are you going to fit in?
- Will you do the job?

What every employer wants?

There are certain personal traits and behaviours that every employer will expect their employees to have. They may not explicitly state that they are looking for these, but they will be looking for clues in your CV and in your whole approach to your job search, that you understand what those desirable behaviours are, and that you can deliver them.

WANTED...

- Ability to handle pressure and conflict
- Energy, enthusiasm, initiative

- Ability to learn
- Hard-working

- Adaptable to change
- Honesty

- Care about quality of work
- Professional approach

- Communication skills
- Reliability

- Confidentiality
- Represents the company well

- Customer service approach
- Team player

PROVING YOU ARE A MODEL EMPLOYEE

So how can you prove on your CV that you have the personal qualities every employer looks for? Use Form 4 to identify some examples of when you have demonstrated these desirable personality traits. They can be everyday activities or more occasional occurrences.

FORM 5: YOUR TRAITS

Every employer wants	Your examples	Tips
Reliability		
Consistently meets deadlines or targets		Ensure CV arrives on time
Willing and ready to work		
Takes on additional tasks if required		
Excellent attendance record and punctuality		Do not claim excellent attendance or punctuality record unless you know that your previous employer will confirm this in their reference
Professionalism		
Takes care in the standard of work		Ensure your CV is well presented and clean, and supplies the information the employer needs
Displays business-appropriate behaviour even under pressure		Your CV will be seen as an illustration of your business approach
Understands business requirements		
Builds constructive working relationships		
Honesty, integrity and confidentiality		
Takes responsibilities of high trust, e.g. money, sensitive matters		Make sure all information supplied in your CV is accurate, including dates and grades

Every employer wants	Your examples	Tips
Deals with confidential information		
Follows an ethical code of practice		
Energy and adaptability		
Takes the initiative		Use positive action words throughout CV, which will give it more of an energetic feel, e.g. led, organised, created
Able to cope with change		
Willing to learn		
Ability to work well within a team		
Role within different team structures, e.g. departmental, external		If you are in a stand-alone role, you need to show you can work independently as well as within a team
Team projects worked on		
Customer service approach		
Represents the company positively		Show on your CV your understanding that customers are both internal and external and both require a customer service focus
Takes care of customers		
Problem-solving approach		
Diplomacy/handling conflict		

Use some of the examples you have identified above in your CV to show your personality 'in action'. The right column in the form shows that the employer will also be making judgements about your personality from the way that your CV is presented. As individuals, we all have our own unique style, preferences and behaviours. Some of these you will be aware of, others may be more unconscious. Your CV is likely to exhibit some of both kinds of characteristics, either overtly, for example in the kinds of achievements you include, or subconsciously, for example in your use of particular words or in how you visually present your CV – an employer is unlikely to believe your examples about your high levels of professionalism if your CV is sloppily presented.

It is therefore worth taking a proactive approach and doing some self-research. You can then identify and make a feature in your CV of some of the particular personality characteristics you have that will be of positive advantage in the role. You can also check (and get someone else to double-check) that any less appropriate traits, for example lack of assertiveness, don't start inadvertently creeping in and affecting the tone of your CV.

Activity 7 will help you start thinking about some of your key personality traits and preferences. Because it is so difficult to be objective about yourself, it is worth asking other people how they view you and seeing if their answers match your own self-perception. Ask them to highlight what they think your personality strengths and behaviours are – and the things you need to watch out for.

> A key point to remember in tailoring your CV is to make sure you communicate a sense of who you are and how you work best. To do this, seek to understand your work style, values and what motivates you at work. This means you can target organisations where you are likely to work well.
>
> *Janet Sheath*
> *Career Consultant*

ACTIVITY 7

YOUR PERSONALITY AND PREFERENCES

Think about the following questions and also ask others for their feedback. Record your thoughts and findings either in this table or separately on paper or on your computer.

- Think of the different teams in which you operate and how you and others would describe your contribution and approach. For example, leader, facilitator, creative, factual, technical, practical, theoretical, etc.

- Do you like working in detail or are you more of a 'big picture' person?

- What is your approach to planning and organising a future activity? Is it structured or more informal?

- Do you like an amount of routine or do you get easily bored?

- How comfortable are you when dealing with issues that are ambiguous, unclear or unstructured?

- How quickly do you tend to make decisions at work?

- How have you handled conflict at work?

- How good are you at persuading and influencing other people?

- How have you coped under pressure?

- How would other people at work describe you?

- How have you dealt with a mistake or a failure you have been responsible for?

- How have you dealt with mistakes made by others that affected you?

- How structured do you like your work to be?

- Do you prefer a logical approach with facts and data to support an argument?

- How much do you use 'gut feel' to make decisions?

- How important to you is it to be physically active in your work?

- How have you coped with change in the past – particularly when it has taken you out of your comfort zone?

- How easy do you find it to talk to new people?

From the information noted above:

1. select the personal characteristics you think are particularly appropriate for your target role and employer
2. think of practical examples of when you have demonstrated these qualities
3. write down up to five examples in the space below that you can use on your CV to show how your personality is an asset. For example: I have the ability to remain calm under pressure as shown by times when I have had to deal with aggressive behaviour from members of the public.

Examples that show my personality/work style in a positive light:

1.
2.
3.
4.
5.

Personality testing or 'testing' personality?

There is a whole industry devoted to helping employers assess whether your psychological profile is the right one for their organisation. Personality testing, usually completed via online questionnaires, is often used in graduate recruitment, where the individual's capabilities and approach are relatively unproven. Organisations may also test candidates for certain jobs where they are looking for specific types of behaviour, for example stress resilience for high-pressure roles.

Personality tests have no right or wrong answers but reflect how a person taking the test would typically act or think.

It is beyond the scope of this book to provide detailed information on personality testing, but as we have seen, all employers will be categorising you to some extent on how well they think your personality fits the role/organisation.

If you are due to take a personality test as part of a forthcoming process or you simply want to do some more self-research, check out the following websites for more information. Most have sample practice tests, many of which you can try for free.

- www.shldirect.com: free practice personality assessments from one of the UK's largest test publishers, including sample questions for OPQ (Occupational Personality Questionnaire)
- www.keirsey.com: complete the free online personality questionnaires: Keirsey Character Sorter and Keirsey Temperament Sorter
- www.teamtechnology.co.uk: free practice personality test drawing on MBTI (Myers-Briggs Type Indicator).

As with aptitude tests, if you are considering paying for any kind of personality test, it is highly recommended that you check out the British Psychological Society website (www.psychtesting.org.uk) for information and guidance.

> Personality at work is all about 'how' you go about doing your job – are you practical or theoretical? Will you follow your own approach regardless, or go along with the majority? Do you prefer to be around others all the time, or do you value your own space more? In this way, personality is an essential part of fitting people to jobs. Personality questionnaires are designed to assess a candidate's perception of their typical or preferred behavioural style. They can focus specifically on a person's behaviour in the workplace and therefore give an indication of likely performance at work and an objective perspective on a person's suitability for a particular role.
>
> *Howard Grosvenor*
> *Managing Consultant, SHL*

IN A NUTSHELL

This chapter has focused on how your personality is part of the selection criteria for shortlisting and helped you to:

- understand that employers will often make a judgement about your personality on the basis of your CV alone
- recognise how you can influence that perception by using examples within your CV that show your personality in a positive light
- ensure that the image you present is a consistent and genuine one, so that the content and presentation of your CV match the person they will be meeting at the interview.

MATCH-MAKING

CHAPTER 5

How to show you are
the perfect fit

Selling your services

Part 1 of this book helped you identify and prove the skills, knowledge and personal qualities that you can offer an employer. However, this is only one side of the story. You need to make sure there is a buyer for what you want to sell. Thousands of candidates apply each year for roles for which they are undoubtedly capable, only to be rejected because they have failed to show in their CV exactly why they are suitable.

Part 2 is designed to help you ascertain what the employer is really looking for, rather than relying on assumptions. By the end of this section, you will have brought together all of your research and have in place the key justifications for your CV of why you should be hired for the role.

5 HOW TO SHOW YOU ARE THE PERFECT FIT

A role in one organisation can be very different from another with the same job title in another company. Assumptions about what a role may entail can be very misleading. This chapter is going to look at how you can find out what the job involves and what the employer is looking for in a candidate. You can then use this information to present yourself as their ideal new member of staff.

This chapter will help you:

■ decode job advertisements

■ use job descriptions and person specifications effectively

■ research target organisations and their markets

■ research the larger job market for your ideal role

■ use all this information to tailor your CV specifically to the employer's requirements.

R ecruitment is a matching exercise. The easier it is for the employer to match your CV with their requirements, the greater the likelihood you will be shortlisted. So let's look first of all at how we can find out what they are looking for.

Reading job advertisements

When you are looking to understand what an employer wants, then the most obvious place to look first is at the job advertisements. Let's review a couple of job advertisements for a corporate legal secretary. Look at the following job advertisement for a corporate legal secretary and highlight what you think are their main requirements.

Corporate legal secretary
£30,000–£31,000 per annum

Looking for involvement? This exciting role would suit a legal secretary/personal assistant who is looking for just that! The position is working for two dynamic partners who specialise in corporate finance. They are often abroad on business hence they are looking for a very experienced legal secretary with extensive experience of corporate finance within a renowned City or West End law firm.

The ideal candidate will be an excellent communicator as you will be liaising with high-profile clientele. A born organiser is required for this exciting role, as lots of travel arrangements and diary management skills are needed.

Very generous staff benefits on offer: 30-day holiday; subsidised staff restaurant; pension scheme; Bupa health insurance; life insurance; gym membership.

Rise to the challenge and email your CV immediately.

The advertisement seems fairly straightforward and up-front about its requirements. However, if we start to analyse it further what other information can we glean and what implications might there be for writing a CV to apply for this role?

TABLE 4: ANALYSING THE ADVERTISEMENT FOR A CORPORATE LEGAL SECRETARY (1)

Advertisement	Analysis
Corporate legal secretary: £30,000–£31,000 per annum	Salary level indicates the seniority level for the job. If seniority level unclear, check on internet and benchmark salary with other jobs to see how it compares
Looking for involvement? Then this exciting role would really suit a legal secretary/ personal assistant who is looking for just that!	This suggests they want someone with initiative and energy who is willing to take responsibility rather than waiting to be told what to do
The position is working for two dynamic partners who specialise in corporate finance	This relationship is key to the role. They will want someone capable of building a strong trusted relationship with the partners. Use examples on CV of previous close working relationships with other managers. Given that relationships take some time to build, they will probably want someone prepared to be around for the longer term. The use of the word 'dynamic' in this context also suggests high energy, demanding pace, and changeable situations. Emphasise in CV about how you are used to working in such environments
They are often abroad on business…	Think of examples where you had to hold the fort while your manager was absent, e.g. sickness, in meetings or where your boss was frequently out of the office. Their absence means that you need to present a confident, highly professional image as well as being self-reliant and able to work on your own initiative
… hence they are looking for a very experienced legal secretary	State legal secretary qualifications early in CV with the number of years of experience.
… with extensive experience of corporate finance	Need to highlight prominently any experience you have of working in these areas, even if this was a relatively small part of what you were doing previously. If you have no experience in this area, then they may not consider you unless you can show them that you have transferable knowledge in this area
… within a renowned City or West End law firm…	If you have not worked within a well-known City/West End firm before, they may not consider you. However, any examples you can give of working in a similar quality, first class, legal organisation may be helpful
The ideal candidate will be an excellent communicator…	State examples of where you have had to communicate with different audiences, e.g. clients, suppliers, other departments, external bodies. Be specific about communication skills used, e.g. answering queries from clients, writing legal correspondences, taking minutes, etc.
… as you will be liaising with high-profile clientele	State any experience working with 'very important persons' (VIPs), not necessarily their names if you need to keep those confidential, but their status, e.g. senior business leader, key figure in entertainment industry

(continued)

(continued)

Advertisement	Analysis
Also, a born organiser is required for this exciting role as lots of travel arrangements and diary management skills is needed.	Even if this was a relatively small part of previous jobs, use separate bullet points to give examples of travel and diary arrangements experience
Very generous staff benefits on offer: 30-day holiday; subsidised staff restaurant; pension scheme; Bupa health insurance; life insurance; gym membership	They want to attract and retain good-quality staff so they are offering good benefits. Make sure that in your CV, it comes over that you are someone looking for a long-term role
Rise to the challenge and email your CV immediately	The whole style of the advertisement is upbeat, dynamic and fast paced. Match this style by using positive action words on your CV to reinforce that you have the energy for the job, e.g. led, organised, created

As you can see, there is lots of information packed in a relatively short advertisement. So for this role, the advice would be that your CV and covering letter should focus on:

- relevant legal qualifications
- previous role with City law firm or similar prestigious legal organisation
- specific experience/knowledge of corporate finance
- experience of liaising with VIP clients
- specific verbal and written communication skills, e.g. accurate message-taking, liaison between partners and clients
- experience of acting as representative for manager or others
- strong secretarial skills including diary management
- experience of organising travel
- IT skills
- use of active, high-energy words throughout the CV to show that you are the right personality for the job.

Now let's compare this with another job for a corporate legal secretary. Same job title, so how different can it be?

> ## Corporate legal secretary, WC1
>
> An experienced, versatile and efficient legal secretary with strong corporate finance experience is urgently required to join this mid-sized commercial law firm based in Central London, where your fast typing and experience in churning out lengthy documents will be highly regarded.
>
> Strong Word and typing skills and command of English grammar is essential. Knowledge of DeltaView and billing is desirable.
>
> If you are looking for work–life balance within a professional environment, then please email us for immediate consideration.

TABLE 5: ANALYSING THE ADVERTISEMENT FOR A CORPORATE LEGAL SECRETARY (2)

Advertisement	Analysis
Corporate legal secretary WC1	As there is no salary advertised it is more difficult to gauge the level at which the job is pitched
An experienced... versatile... and efficient... legal secretary	State how many years' experience you have as a legal secretary. Versatile could mean varied organisational duties or it could just mean that you get asked to make the tea. In your CV show your flexibility, your duties involving welcoming visitors, liaising with IT, etc. Efficient – important to convey your speed and accuracy. Use words such as 'quickly, fast turnaround'. State your legal qualifications in full
... with strong corporate finance experience	State in your career profile your corporate finance experience. If you do not have this or any directly related experience, they may not shortlist you
... is urgently required to join this mid-sized commercial law firm based in Central London	They may be prepared to be flexible on some of their selection criteria if you can start soon. State your availability – especially if it is immediate
... where your fast typing, and experience in churning out lengthy documents will be highly regarded	State your typing speeds. Emphasise your fast working and give examples of meeting deadlines. Give examples of the type of long documents you have produced. This is clearly the central part of the job

(continued)

(continued)

Advertisement	Analysis
Strong Word and typing skills… and command of English grammar essential	State that you have excellent Word and typing skills – however, only apply for this role if this is true as it is such a key component of the job that they are likely to test this at the interview. Include on CV any English academic qualifications and specify your grades if they were especially good. Ensure the spelling and grammar in your CV and covering letter are perfect.
Knowledge of Deltaview and billing is desirable	State your experience of DeltaView in your career profile. If you do not have this experience, find out specifically about DeltaView and then draw on any transferable knowledge you may have, e.g. 'I have extensive experience of ABC, which is a comparable system to DeltaView and am confident that as a fast learner, I can pick up and apply DeltaView very quickly.' Equally state billing experience and knowledge
If you are looking for work–life balance within a professional environment, then…	The work–life balance is an important statement as it implies that you should be able to go home on time – not always the case in law firms
… please email us for immediate consideration	The 'immediate' reinforces their need for someone quickly. Send them your CV as soon as possible, as they are likely to recruit the first suitable candidate

When responding to this advertisement, the key requirements that should be focused on are:

- relevant legal qualifications
- corporate finance experience
- typing speeds, e.g. of producing long documents against tight deadlines, able to work quickly and efficiently
- immediate availability
- good written English skill
- knowledge of Dataview or equivalent
- knowledge and experience of billing
- applying as quickly as possible.

You can see from the two legal secretary examples that although these are both advertisements for jobs with the same title, there are very different expectations of the post-holder. This shows how important it is to avoid making assumptions about what you think the job is. Try to gain as much information as you can to help you tailor your CV to what the employer really wants.

Job descriptions and person specification forms

More detailed information on a particular job is often given in a job description and person specification form. These are usually, but not always, made available to candidates before they apply for the post – either the organisation will send it to you or you can access it via its website. It is always worth asking if there is one available for you to look at because although job descriptions will vary in the amount of detail provided, their aim is to tell you exactly what the employer wants. This makes your task of matching their requirements on your CV much more straightforward.

Recruitment agencies may not always supply this information either because they don't have it or because they are trying to protect the employer's anonymity or their commission. However, it is always worth asking them if there is a copy they could send.

Job description

This will usually list the job duties, responsibilities and reporting structure for the role. You can see the kind of activities you will be involved in as well as any people management and financial responsibilities. Organisations will have their own format for their job descriptions and all their recruitment forms but they will usually look something like the examples given here.

SAMPLE JOB DESCRIPTION

Client side developer
Reporting to: Client side manager
Location: Pulham
Staff reports: None

Gladstone Computer Technologies is looking for an experienced, professional and enthusiastic front-end developer to join a world-class team.

Key responsibilities

- To write complex code using semantic X/HTML, CSS, object-oriented JavaScript and other equivalent client side technologies.
- To liaise with the product manager to ensure that all technical possibilities are explored and that products achieve the best possible look, feel and functionality.
- To work with designers and software engineers to ensure that interactive elements of designs work.
- To work with all relevant parties on the deployment of code to the live site.
- To monitor work against the production schedule closely and provide progress updates and report any issues or technical difficulties to the Senior Client Side Developer on a regular basis.

The person specification (Table 6) is usually attached to the job description and it summarises the criteria that the employer will use to determine whether you meet the shortlisting requirements.

TABLE 6: SAMPLE PERSON SPECIFICATION CRITERIA FOR CLIENT SIDE DEVELOPER	Essential – E Desirable – D
Knowledge	
Knowledge of semantic X/HTML, JavaScript and CSS	E
Experience of commercial web development processes	E
Working knowledge of JavaScript libraries, XSLT/XML, Flash/ActionScript, Template Toolkit, PHP	E
Knowledge of information architecture principles and techniques	D
Qualifications and training	
Relevant degree	D
Appropriate web development qualifications/training	E
Key competencies	
Ability to simplify complex problems or projects into component parts, exploring and evaluating them systematically, and identifying and resolving problems	E
Ability to present well-reasoned arguments to effectively convince others	E
Able to take initiative, taking a proactive approach to work without close supervision	E
Ability to communicate with technical and non-technical audiences	E
High-performance working under the pressure of demanding deadlines	E

The person(s) responsible for shortlisting candidates will either use the person specification form as shown in Table 6 or they will have a slightly amended form like the following one, which they will use to assess each candidate's CV.

TABLE 7: SAMPLE PERSON SPECIFICATION CRITERIA FOR CLIENT SIDE DEVELOPER

		Assessment method	
	Essential – E Desirable – D	CV	Interview
Knowledge			
Knowledge of semantic X/HTML, JavaScript and CSS	E	☐	☐
Experience of commercial web development processes	E	☐	☐
Working knowledge of JavaScript libraries, XSLT/XML, Flash/ActionScript, Template Toolkit, PHP	E	☐	☐
Knowledge of information architecture principles and techniques	D	☐	☐
Qualifications and training			
Relevant degree	D	☐	☐
Appropriate web development qualifications	E	☐	☐
Key competencies			
Ability to simplify complex problems or projects into component parts, exploring and evaluating them systematically, and identifying and resolving problems	E	☐	☐
Ability to present well-reasoned arguments to effectively convince others	E	☐	☐
Able to take initiative, taking a proactive approach to work without close supervision	E	☐	☐
Ability to communicate with technical and non-technical audiences	E	☐	☐
High performance working under the pressure of demanding deadlines	E	☐	☐

As you can see from the forms, shortlisting is a systematic process whereby a 'tick' is obtained only if you have proved on your CV that you meet the specific requirement the employer is looking for. The more ticks you get, the more likely you are to be shortlisted.

Many good candidates fail to get on the shortlist pile because they make assumptions about what employers will 'read into' a CV. For instance, consider an experienced secretary who is applying for a role where diary management skills are a key requirement. They feel that the employer will know that diary management was a key part of their last job and so they do not itemise it separately. However, the employer's perception is likely to be that secretarial roles vary greatly and if the candidate has not made explicit reference to diary management skills, it is an

TABLE 8: ADAPTING YOUR CV TO DIFFERENT TYPES OF ORGANISATIONAL CULTURE

Organisational culture	Emphasise in your CV
Bureaucratic	
Importance of following processes, rules, procedures, paperwork, e.g. civil service	Activities involving rules, policies and procedures that needed to be followed
	Applications that have needed to be completed for achievements of quality standards, accreditations, awards, grants, etc.
	Membership of committees, institutes
	Any liaison with trade unions, professional bodies
	Compliance activities, e.g. helping the organisation meet legal, health and safety, and financial obligations
Altruistic	
Focus is on a higher value, i.e. an outcome that is other than monetary gain, e.g. charity organisation	Your strong identification with the organisation's service, product or cause
	Emphasise voluntary work or community activities undertaken, e.g. fundraising, charity committees
	Achievements should focus on quality outcomes as well as financial ones
Entrepreneurial	
Innovative, risk taking, quick to act upon opportunities, e.g. business start-ups	Use words such as initiated, created, identified
	Include examples of where you came up with an idea which worked
	Emphasise speed, tight timescales, the need to act quickly
	Talk about how you have helped identify opportunities, helped the business to grow, return on investment
	Show how you have helped your employers make money, retain or win new customers
	Highlight strong commercial and business acumen
	Mention any dealings with external investors
Expert culture	
Organisations where knowledge is prized, e.g. universities	Highlight particular expertise, qualifications, technical knowledge, specialisms, sector insight, professional memberships
	Emphasise your continuous updating of knowledge, learning and development activities
	Include examples of when your advice was sought both internally and externally
	Reports, recommendations, books, publications, guidance materials, manuals produced

Organisational culture	Emphasise in your CV
Task culture	
Project based/ action orientated, team approach, e.g. management consultancy	Emphasise involvement with tasks/projects and their outcomes
	Include lots of examples of working in a team, including cross-department or cross-organisational
	Focus on objective and goal-setting activities and their achievement
	Influencing skills, time-management skills, matrix working-structures
	Examples of building a team, supervising, organisational abilities, handling conflict
Power culture	
Organisations where decisions made quickly either by one person or a few key players with little or no consultation, e.g. some family businesses	Include examples of being asked by your manager/chief executive officer (CEO) to lead an activity, work on a project
	Highlight close working relationships
	Give examples of briefing senior management team/CEO
Creative	
Where ideas, originality, aesthetics are important, e.g. advertising, publishing	CV design should be visually pleasing and look different from a standard CV. Perhaps use PDF or web CV (see Chapter 11)
	Include ideas you have proposed and outcomes
	Include more creative hobbies and interests
	Show how up to date you are in your field, refer to industry trends
	Let your personality come through on CV, your approach to your work
	Use the jargon appropriate for the organisation/industry
Reward culture	
Where staff are rewarded for performance rather than length of service, e.g. sales-driven organisations	Focus on performance targets which have been met
	Include examples of any awards, recognition or positive feedback from management, customers
	Examples of how you have added value to the organisation, e.g. new customers, repeat business
	Use energy, action-orientated words such as led, initiated
Strategic	
Focused on longer-term objectives, e.g. economic think tank	Emphasise research and planning approach to activities
	Include examples of longer-term gains achieved
	Include change management activities, e.g. reviewing work processes, restructuring responsibilities

Organisational culture	Emphasise in your CV
Short-term focus	
Organisations focused on the here and now, e.g. telesales organisations	Use 'energy' words and phrases such as fast-paced, quick turnaround
	Focus on results achieved within short timescales
	Emphasis short-term projects

There are many other types of organisational culture, but once you become attuned to what to look for, then you can weave hints into your CV that show you understand and can fit in with how the organisation operates.

Researching the employer's market

You only need to read the business news to see how organisations are continually adjusting to external pressures whether it is a market downturn, new opportunities, competitive pressures, etc.

An organisation's staff requirements will depend, for instance, on whether it's looking to grow the business, trying to keep its head above the water or needing to innovate to stay ahead. You can use this information to good effect on your CV by focusing on those areas likely to be important for the future, e.g. your international experience because you can see they are looking to grow their business abroad.

ACTIVITY 9

ANALYSING AN EMPLOYER'S MARKETPLACE

- Is the employer's product or service in a market that is buoyant or in recession?

- Who is the market leader in its sector and how does this company compare with competitors?

- What does the organisation see as its competitive edge?

- Who are the target customers?

- What are the greatest challenges, opportunities and threats in the sector?

- What are the projected trends in the market for the future?

- What will it need from its employees in the future?

Understanding where the organisation is in relation to those external pressures will help you anticipate what the employer may be looking for right now, as well as for the future. If you are going to post your CV on an internet recruitment site or send it speculatively to employers on the off-chance that they may have a suitable job, then you need to do your research slightly differently, as shown in Activity 10.

ACTIVITY 10

RESEARCHING THE JOB MARKET

First, aim to find five to six advertisements for jobs similar to the one that you are looking for and try to determine the following employer requirements from the information provided:

- Skills, knowledge and experience
- Qualifications/training
- Personal characteristics

- Salary range
- Key duties and responsibilities
- Any other particular requirements.

Second:

- Talk to people you know, ideally managers, who are working in your chosen field. Ask their opinion on the recruitment market and what they would look for in a potential employee for this role.

- Ask recruitment agencies – they are on the front line and can tell you what skills are in demand and what differentiates the successful candidates.

- Check whether your professional association or trade journal monitors recruitment trends for its members – many do.

- Search the internet for online salary surveys, of which there are many. Simply type in 'salary survey' and your job title or sector into a search engine and this is likely to bring up some good examples.

- NB: internet job sites can give a false impression of the supply of actual jobs because some recruitment agencies advertise in more than one place or don't remove filled jobs from their lists of available jobs. See Chapter 16 for more details. Advertisements that have been placed by or on behalf of named employers are more likely to be reliable.

Third, use this information to help you:

- Check whether you are being realistic in what you are looking for

- Identify the common recruitment requirements for your target role and show how you meet these in your CV

- Focus your energy on sending your speculative CV to the sectors most likely to be recruiting for your type of skills

- Ascertain if there is anything else that you could do to give yourself a competitive edge. If so, go out and do it and then highlight it on your CV

- Benchmark the salary levels so that you know what you are worth and can negotiate.

WHO IS THE IDEAL CANDIDATE?

Gather all of your research from this chapter and record it in Form 6 to identify the employer's ideal candidate. You can use the form given here or create it separately on paper or on your computer.

Record your research findings on your target job(s) from:

- Job advertisements, job descriptions and person specification forms

- Talking to people who know the target job(s) or organisations

- Getting feedback from agencies on the current market for this type of job

- Benchmarking to compare with similar jobs in different organisations

- Viewing the employer's website, their marketing material, core values, etc.

- Finding out what is happening in the employer's market or the sector generally

- Comparing target organisations with their competitors.

FORM 6: THE IDEAL CANDIDATE

	The ideal candidate will have:
Skills/competencies	
Experience	
Knowledge	
Education/qualifications	
Training	
Personal characteristics, e.g. personal qualities, working style	
Organisational characteristics, e.g. bureaucratic	
Any other requirements, e.g. professional memberships	

MATCHING YOU TO THE ROLE

Use your research from Part 1 and the findings from Activity 10 to show how you can prove to the employer that you are the ideal candidate. If there are any areas that don't match, identify what you can do right now or in the future to bridge any gaps in suitability.

FORM 7: SHOW YOU'RE THE IDEAL CANDIDATE

Key requirements (see notes from Activity 11)	Examples of how you meet the requirements	Are there any gaps? If so how are you going to bridge them? For example, training, voluntary work, reading, secondment, work-shadowing, enrolling on a course

IN A NUTSHELL

This chapter has focused on the different ways you can research what an employer is looking for in a candidate. It has helped you to:

■ check rather than assume that you know who the employer's ideal candidate is
■ provide examples of how you meet their stated selection criteria
■ identify other aspects that might influence candidate selection
■ identify gaps and work out how you might bridge them.

DEVISING YOUR CV

What should your CV look and sound like?

Parts 1 and 2 of this book helped you evolve the content for your CV. Now you need to start writing it and putting the content into shape.

Part 3 is going to focus on the form, structure and tone of your CV. It will show you how different headings and formats for your CV can be used to make it easier for you to organise the information and for the employer to appreciate your suitability for the post.

Although you will find many different views on what a CV should look like, the truth is that as long as you follow three simple rules, there is flexibility in how you choose to display your CV.

Three rules for a winning CV

- Your CV should be well presented, clean and professional.
- Essential information such as your contact details, career history and relevant qualifications should be included.
- It should be easy for the employer to see why you are a suitable candidate.

Let's look at how we can help you achieve this.

6 THE FIRST HALF PAGE OF YOUR CV

This is the most important part of your CV because it will determine whether the rest of it is read by the employer or not. You need to create an opening for your CV that is functional and smart, and gains the employer's interest.

This chapter will help you:

- select an appropriate title for your CV

- ensure your contact details are complete, appropriate and functional

- write a career profile and career objective statement that will grab the employer's attention.

Your CV is essentially a sales document. The aim is to generate the employer's interest so that they will invite you to an interview. You are competing not only with other applicants but also with other demands on an employer's time. Typically an employer will scan your CV in less than 15 seconds, paying most attention to the top half of the first page. If you grab their attention early on with lots of relevant information, then they are likely to read through the rest of the CV. If you bury all of the relevant experience on page 2, then there is no guarantee that they will read that far before placing you on the reject pile.

Let's look at how you can make the first half page work in your favour.

CV headings

Curriculum vitae/résumé?

There is one heading that you are not going to need. Do not head your CV with either Curriculum Vitae or Résumé. It's not wrong, just old-fashioned. There is also a danger that if this is the first heading on your CV a computer could scan your name as 'Mr Curriculum Vitae'.

> If I can make one simple plea to anyone writing a CV, it is to remember that it is a marketing tool not an autobiography. When applying for a role, ensure that everything on your CV sells you for that job. I do not want to spend time looking for some hint of why an individual is applying for a particular job.
>
> *Cathy Earle*
> *Head of Human Resources*

Personal information

Your name

This should always be at the very top of your CV, usually in a bigger font than the rest of the CV, for example, size 14 if you are using 12 elsewhere. You could also use capital letters.

Always include your name as a footer at the bottom of the CV with the page number and the total number of pages. This way, if any pages become detached as they often do during photocopying, they can easily be reassembled.

Address

Always include a contact address if you are sending your CV directly to an employer. If you leave this out, then an employer will wonder where you are located, whether you have a permanent address at all and therefore how ready you are to start working for them.

However, recruitment agencies will usually leave your contact details out to ensure that all offers from an employer come through them rather than directly to the individual.

If you are posting your CV online in a public forum then you may want to include just your email address rather than all of your personal contact information, in order to maintain privacy and safety.

Telephone number

It is now acceptable just to provide your mobile number if this is the best number to contact you on. Remember not to give your current work telephone number as a contact number unless your manager is aware that you are looking for a new job. It is too risky.

Email address

Use an individual personal email address for your job-searching activities rather than your current work email address or a shared address. Set up a free Gmail, Hotmail or Yahoo address if needed (see p. 7).

UK rights to work

You need only state this if your background and experience is clearly non-EU.

What you shouldn't include

Don't include any of the following:

- date of birth
- religion
- sex
- marital status
- number of children
- disabilities
- political affiliations.

Examples of layout for personal information

Hanif Kotecha

58 Elms Avenue, Sawbridge

SW9 ABC

Mobile: 0777 777 555

Email: hk@hotmail.com

Footer:

CV   H. Kotecha   page 1 of 2

John Brown

Address:	7983 South Boulevard, Gladstown, South Africa
Mobile:	+44 0777 666 555
Email:	johnb@yahoo.com
Work status:	Approved to work in UK under the Highly Skilled Migrant Programme

Footer:

CV   John Brown   1/2

Writing a career profile

A career profile is a mini-advertisement that is placed directly after your personal details to try to capture the attention of the employer and summarise why you are a great candidate. It consists of approximately three to five sentences describing the skills, knowledge and experience you have that are relevant to the job sought. It usually sits in its own section on the first page, situated directly under the personal contact details. A career profile is optional, but used thoughtfully, it can be very effective to quickly create a positive first impression.

So what should go in a career profile?

Job title

Employees can get very hot under the collar about job titles and what they feel their role should be called. However, job titles are notoriously misleading. There is no standardisation across organisations about job titles. Even departments within the same organisation will often use job titles differently. Recruiters will look to confirm the seniority of your role by looking at your salary, scope of responsibilities, staff responsibilities, etc. rather than your job title alone.

However, given this, wherever possible, use the title of the job you are applying for, to describe yourself within the career profile. If they are looking for a 'customer services assistant', then call yourself this even if your previous job title was actually 'customer liaison officer'. This is justifiable if your previous roles have been similar in function. Psychologically, if the recruiter sees a candidate with the right job label in the career profile, even if your job title is listed differently in your career history, then they are more likely to believe in your suitability. Of course this has to be substantiated by the rest of your CV. It's no use calling yourself 'customer services manager' when your CV shows no evidence of management skills.

Key experience

The career profile should include how many years' experience you have in the area they are looking for. For example:

- *sales adviser with over 20 years' sales experience within the computer retail sector.*
- *5 years' post-qualification experience internationally as a chartered surveyor.*
- *10 years' experience working as a technical engineer within the UK telecommunications sector.*

Relevant qualifications, education, professional affiliations

Where professional qualifications are required, put these in the profile. For example:

- CIMA qualified accountant
- RCIS qualified surveyor
- part-qualified paralegal secretary
- Full Member of the Chartered Institute of Purchasing and Supply (MCIPS)
- Associate Fellow of the British Psychological Society
- MSc in Engineering

You can also include relevant degrees, e.g. MBA, and/or chartered status if you belong to a professional institute.

Key knowledge

Itemise any relevant specialist knowledge you have:

- industry expert on network architecture
- specialist in crime prevention for businesses
- excellent knowledge of arboriculture.

Relevant training

Include any training that supports your work:

- trained mediator
- trained in health and safety risk assessments
- trained in CAD design.

Personal attributes

As we have seen in Part 1, employers do like to get a sense of what you are like as a person/employee.

Many candidates will include in their career profile some personality traits which they think will impress the employer. Some attributes that frequently appear on CVs are: dynamic, charismatic, team player, excellent communicator, hard-working, visionary, capable, dependable, people person, innovative.

However, without evidence to back these up, they are pretty meaningless. There is also a real danger that if you go over the top, it can have a counter-productive effect. The most over-used phrases in career profiles are 'good communication skills' and 'team player'. This isn't going to give you much of a competitive edge as 99.9% of candidates assume, rightly or wrongly, that they have these attributes. However, specifying what type of communication skills you have can be an important differentiator (Table 9).

TABLE 9: INSTEAD OF 'STRONG COMMUNICATION SKILLS' SPECIFY THE TYPE OF COMMUNICATION SKILLS YOU HAVE

Verbal	Written
Persuading individuals	Writing correspondence
Influencing stake-holders	Writing reports
Selling to customers	Accurate message taking
Presenting to an audience	Shorthand
Mediating conflict	Summarising information
Negotiating in person	Presenting research findings
Dealing with complaints	Writing copy for promotional materials
Making visitors feel welcome	Producing technical manuals
Relationship building	Filling in forms
Articulating needs	Producing newsletters
Translating	Transcribing
Advocacy	Writing policies and procedures
Training	Proof-reading

Review your research in Parts 1 and 2 of this book. What kind of person is the employer looking for? Focus on identifying the particular interpersonal skills and abilities that you think they want and provide evidence to demonstrate that you have them. For example:

- strong relationship-building skills that have resulted in three of our biggest customers increasing their orders by 25%
- used to dealing with confidential and sensitive information while secretary for the executive board meetings
- highly creative thinker whose innovative presentation ideas have attracted new customers such as Jonas Lighting, Gladhouse Electricals, The Bulb Company.

You can use words such as 'results orientated' or 'commercially focused' only if your CV includes examples of where you achieved concrete goals and/or made money for the company. Equally, if you are using words such as dynamic then your CV should back this up, for example fast-track promotions, new customers won, changes implemented, awards, etc. Unless your CV shows evidence of this, then 'dynamic' is going to look more of a wish than a reality. So remember, any trait used in the career profile must be borne out by the rest of your CV.

TABLE 10: IDENTIFY PARTICULAR INTERPERSONAL SKILLS AND ABILITIES

Good negotiator ✘	Highly experienced in negotiating favourable contract terms with software suppliers ✓
Strong communication skills ✘	Highly developed interpersonal skills acquired as a result of working with individuals under stress ✓
Excellent written skills ✘	Adept at liaising between technical and non-technical staff to produce user-friendly guidance materials ✓

EXAMPLES OF CAREER PROFILES

■ Industry award-winning Marketing Director with over 15 years' experience of working in the consumer food industry. Proven track record in turning under-performing brands into market leaders within very short timescales. Responsible for many innovative and successful new product launches, e.g. Double Chocolate Cookies, which took 15% market share within 12 weeks against a dominant market leader.

■ Chartered Institute of Personnel and Development (CIPD)-qualified human resources (HR) officer with over 3 years' experience of working in the public sector. Used to working closely with line managers on a wide range of HR issues, including staff recruitment and disciplinary and grievance handling. Excellent interpersonal skills, particularly in dealing with sensitive issues such as redundancy situations.

■ Technical operations manager with over 10 years' experience of working with fast-paced organisations in the telecommunications market with X-mobile. Highly knowledgeable about new and emerging technologies and used to managing the roll-out of new products from inception to delivery in-store. Used to managing both technical and people resources to deliver complex projects within demanding timescales, e.g. the up-scaling of all mobile web-based technologies within a 6-month period.

■ 4 years' experience as a graphic designer working for prestigious, image-aware organisations such as the Creative Solutions Group. Specialist areas include the redesign and branding of annual reports, sales and marketing information and ensuring brand consistency throughout the organisation. Enjoy working as part of a creative team to innovate and refresh an organisation's visual messages.

Additional information

Think of anything else that you can put in the career profile that will make you stand out from the crowd.

- Have you won any awards?
- Do you speak relevant languages?
- Have you created something well known?
- Did you work for prestigious companies, individuals or projects?
- Have you appeared in the media in your professional capacity?
- Have you published any research or books?

If there is something that is particularly impressive or even quirky that shows you in a good light, include this in the career profile.

Writing a career objective statement

A career objective statement can be used either as part of or instead of a career profile statement. Simply put, it says what kind of job you are looking for and why. Opinions vary as to their usefulness and they do seem to be more common outside the UK and for certain candidate groups such as first-time employees.

A career objective statement is particularly helpful when:

- you have just left school or university and have little or no work experience
- you are applying to a company with lots of potential routes
- you don't want to be pigeon-holed in the area that your CV suggests
- you are applying for promotion and want to justify why you are suitable even if you do not have all of the experience required for working at the new level
- you are posting your CV on a public website and want to be clear about the kinds of roles you are interested in
- you are sending your CV speculatively to organisations.

Some typical examples of career objective statements are given below.

- Experienced programme developer seeking a role that requires extensive liaison between technical teams and non-technical end-users.
- Technical Project Manager looking for a management position that utilises my analytical and organisational skills alongside my people management abilities.

■ Following completion of my Certificate in CIPD, I am looking for a role in an HR department where my substantial administrative skills can help me further my career in the HR field.

The disadvantage of career objective statements is that if you state too narrow a job focus, it could mean that you exclude yourself from other potentially interesting opportunities which the employer could have in mind. Also, if you choose to include a career objective statement, then make sure that the job you say you are looking for, is compatible with the one for which you have just applied.

CAREER PROFILE VERSUS CAREER OBJECTIVE STATEMENTS

Career profile: Useful attention-grabber highlighting your suitability

■ Use if role is relevant to previous career history

■ Can help you keep your options open

■ Use on a speculative CV if you want to avoid narrowing your options.

Career objective: Use if you want to be considered only for specific roles or employers

■ Provides opportunity to justify why ready for promotion

■ Can use to highlight transferability of skills if changing career direction

■ Use to explain that looking for first job/ graduate entry role

■ Can highlight your wish to work for a particular employer rather than a defined role

■ Use if expressly asked for by employer

■ More commonly used in some countries than others, e.g. USA.

NB: You can always combine the two. This enables you to retain the attractive sales pitch of the career profile while being clear about the roles you are interested in.

WRITING A CAREER PROFILE/ CAREER OBJECTIVE STATEMENT

Choose whether you are going to write a career profile or career objective statement or a combination of the two. Write your statement in the space provided or separately on your computer.

1　Look through your research from Part 1 of this book to help you cherry-pick your relevant career experience, significant achievements and personal qualities.

2　Review your research from Part 2 of this book to focus on your target employer's key requirements. Aim to show in your statement how you meet these.

3　Use three to five carefully chosen sentences with a confident tone.

4　Use job title to describe yourself in a way that is relevant to the job sought and which you can justify.

5　Remember to keep all claims factual and specific and consistent with the rest of your CV.

6　Do not refer to yourself in third person.

7　Be realistic if stating the role you are looking for next.

Speaking volumes

The language you use in your CV works on many different levels. It:

- conveys factual content
- directly and indirectly expresses what the individual thinks about that content
- creates associations for the reader, some of which are fairly predictable whereas others will be more personal to the individual.

Most importantly, careful and deliberate use of language in your CV can influence all three points in your favour.

This chapter looks at how you can use language cleverly within your CV to not only convey the factual information but to reinforce an image in the employer's eye of you as an ideal candidate.

Me, myself and I: using the personal pronoun

How you refer to yourself within the CV is going to influence what the reader thinks about you and how they think you view yourself. So choose wisely.

The 'I' option

This is used for a more formal approach, when you are writing in full sentences. However, it usually means that you have to repeatedly use the personal pronoun as in 'I did this' and 'I was responsible for that', which tends to look clumsy, egocentric and quickly becomes tiresome to read.

The 'We' option

Within an organisation, people frequently use the word 'we' in conversations as there is often an emphasis on team and organisational teamwork. However, in recruitment, the employer is interested in what *you* did. If you use the pronoun 'we' within your CV or the interview, then it becomes unclear what contribution you made.

The third person option

Some CVs refer to the individual in the third person as though someone else has written the CV on their behalf, e.g. 'Jones spent 10 years working with...'.

If you are thinking of writing it in this style then be careful. It frequently trips people up and they get themselves in all kinds of grammatical confusions and then start using the 'I' pronoun later on. There can also be a tendency to pile on the superlatives, e.g. 'Jones is a master of his craft…'. However, most of the time we know Jones has written it and it makes him look like a complete egomaniac.

It is appropriate to use this option if someone else really is writing it for you, e.g. a head-hunter creating a profile for you or something produced by your organisation as part of their sales and marketing, e.g. management consultancy.

No pronoun

Perhaps the easiest solution is to try to avoid personal pronouns altogether. Rather than writing full sentences, the use of bullet points led by strong action words reduces the need for any pronoun at all. The advantages of bullet points over full formal sentences are given below.

BULLET POINTS VERSUS FULL SENTENCES

■ Won a £2 million contract for new service arrangements by leading the bid team. Responsibility for writing and presenting the contract bid and project-managed its successful implementation within an ambitious 6-month time-frame.

or

I was responsible for the project team which won the £2 million pound contract for new service arrangements. Appointed to lead the team, I was involved in writing the contract proposal and I also presented the bid. I was then asked to manage the implementation of the new arrangements which I successfully achieved within an ambitious 6-month time-frame required by the customer.

Which do you think works best?

The bullet point is clean and succinct with no personal pronoun. The paragraph is longer, clumsier, repeatedly uses 'I' and full sentences which makes it seem long-winded. In the words of the Elvis song '*A little less conversation and a little more action*' will stand you in good stead.

Choose bullet points without personal pronouns, to make your message in an action-orientated and economical way.

The magic of words

A study by the psychology department of University of Hertfordshire in 2005 showed that specific words and phrases used in CVs and application forms were a key influence in determining which candidates were shortlisted.

TABLE 11: UNIVERSITY OF HERTFORDSHIRE 2005 STUDY, WORDS TO INCLUDE IN A CV	
Top 10 words to include	**Top 10 words to exclude**
Achievement	Always
Active	Awful
Developed	Bad
Evidence	Fault
Experience	Hate
Impact	Mistake
Individual	Never
Involved	Nothing
Planning	Panic
Transferable skills	Problems

Every recruiter and admissions office will have to assess hundreds, if not thousands, of personal statements from hopeful applicants and will make their decision based on what they can see on paper. Choosing the right words is, therefore, vitally important if your application is to stand out from the rest.

Karen Pine
Professor of Developmental Psychology, University of Hertfordshire

Here is a list of words that you can sprinkle throughout your CV to help reinforce the message that you are a positive, upbeat, 'can-do' type of candidate – the kind that every employer wants.

Useful action words for your CV

accelerated	authored	completed
accomplished	awarded	constructed
achieved	balanced	contributed
adapted	boosted	controlled
advised	briefed	convinced
advocated	broadened	coordinated
aligned	built	created
allocated	calculated	cultivated
analysed	canvassed	customised
applied	centralised	decreased
arbitrated	chaired	defeated
arranged	clarified	defined
assessed	coached	delivered
attained	collaborated	demonstrated
attracted	communicated	designed
audited	compiled	determined

developed	fixed	minimised
devised	focused	mobilised
diagnosed	forecast	modernised
differentiated	formulated	modified
directed	fortified	monitored
discovered	founded	motivated
disseminated	generated	navigated
distinguished	guided	negotiated
diversified	handled	nurtured
documented	harmonised	operated
doubled	headed	orchestrated
drafted	helped	organised
educated	highlighted	originated
eliminated	identified	outlined
enabled	illustrated	overcame
encouraged	implemented	overhauled
enforced	improved	oversaw
engineered	incorporated	persuaded
enhanced	increased	piloted
enjoyed	influenced	pinpointed
enlarged	initiated	pioneered
enriched	innovated	planned
ensured	inspired	prepared
equipped	instigated	presented
established	integrated	prioritised
evaluated	introduced	promoted
examined	invested	proved
exhibited	investigated	publicised
expanded	launched	published
experimented	led	qualified
explained	liaised	raised
explored	located	ran
extended	managed	recommended
facilitated	marketed	reconciled
filtered	maximised	recruited
finalised	mediated	rectified
fine-tuned	mentored	reduced

refined
regulated
rehabilitated
reinforced
renewed
reorganised
repaired
repaired
replaced
researched
reshaped
resolved
restored
retained
revamped
reviewed
revitalised
saved
scheduled

secured
selected
set goals
set up
shaped
shared
simplified
sold
solved
sorted
spear-headed
specialised
specialised
standardised
straightened
stream-lined
strengthened
structured
summarised

supervised
supported
surpassed
taught
tested
trained
transformed
uncovered
unified
updated
upgraded
utilised
validated
verified
visualised
volunteered
won
wrote

Useful adverbs

accurately
assertively
astutely
capably
carefully
clearly
cleverly
collaboratively
competently
consistently
consultative

cooperatively
creatively
decisively
effectively
efficiently
energetically
enthusiastically
ethically
inclusively
positively
powerfully

proactively
promptly
quickly
rapidly
resourcefully
responsibly
selectively
sensitively
successfully
well-judged

Use these and similar words to describe how you approached your tasks and achievements. The more positive words you can include, the more positive an impression you will create.

Toxic words

In the University of Hertfordshire study, the researchers also identified certain words it was best to avoid in a CV (see Table 11). Interestingly, the words 'always' and 'never' were often viewed by employers as negative because it suggested that the applicant was exaggerating their abilities.

Here are some other words that it is probably best to avoid in your CV, unless you are showing how you achieved a positive from a negative, e.g. 'successfully launched design previously thought unworkable'.

Words to avoid

abandoned	fired	objectionable
absurd	fought	opposed
argued	futile	preposterous
attempted	gave up	recession
avoided	grievance	ridiculous
bullying	harassed	shoddy
bureaucratic	hopeless	slump
closed down	idiotic	stress
confined	impossible	stupid
conflicted	impractical	succumbed
criticised	incapable	tried
decline	inconceivable	ugly
decrease	indecisive	unbearable
defeated	ineffectual	unendurable
denied	inept	unmanageable
difficult	infuriating	unreasonable
disagreement	intolerable	unruly
disciplined	irreparable	unsuccessfully
dismissed	irreversible	unworkable
disorganised	isolated	weak
down-sized	lost	withdrew
empty	maddening	wrestled
exasperating	miserable	
failed	non-viable	

Technical words

Most industries or professional/technical jobs have their own jargon or buzz words. These should be used to show your relevant knowledge. However, often the person shortlisting is not a technical expert, so care needs to be taken that they can understand what you are talking about.

It is safe and desirable to use jargon that has already been used in the job description or advertisement. Where you describe in detail other technical skills or knowledge, make sure that you clearly link it to a particular skill or competence described in the job description or advertisement so a non-technical recruiter can see its relevance.

Pitch perfect

The language used in your CV needs to be positive and confident. However, it also needs to avoid being 'over the top'. How can you judge the difference? Compare these sentences:

- Managed a charity event attended by 100 people that raised £15,000 for charity and generated excellent PR in the local paper for the company
- Superb organiser, fundraiser and event manager. Excellent PR skills.

The first statement is anchored with evidence – you know what the event was, its size and scale and the outcomes. The second sentence may equally be true but there is no evidence provided to back up the claims. Therefore the use of words such as 'superb' and 'fantastic' are seen to reflect only the candidate's view which is unsubstantiated.

As a result the first sentence is credible – the second sentence is 'over-the-top'. Other 'over-the-top' language could include describing yourself as:

- talented
- brilliant
- born leader
- visionary
- wonderful
- the best salesperson in Europe
- the most capable graduate of their generation.

As stand-alone statements, these are highly subjective and unconvincing. On the other hand if these superlatives are true, then you should provide examples of these skills in action, e.g.:

'Achieved the highest sales figures in the entire European department'; 'Led organisation from verge of bankruptcy to profit within three years as a result of re-shaping the business process and developing profitable product lines'; 'Talented designer who won 2008 industry award for best website and received nominations in two other categories'.

Now let's start writing the main body of your CV. The following chapters present a number of different CV formats you can use. Read through the chapters to decide which of these suit you best.

You will now need all the information you have gained from working through the activities in this book.

IN A NUTSHELL

This chapter has focused on helping you choose language that will support and complement the content of your CV. Remember to:

- use positive language throughout your CV, including action-orientated and positive descriptive words, e.g. 'created' or 'sensitively'
- use negative words only if showing how you improved the situation, e.g. 'Achieved 30% sales increase for a product line that had previously performed badly'
- always provide evidence of any claims about your excellent performance
- results-orientated bullet points reinforce the sense of energy in the CV and help avoid the over-use of the 'I' or 'we' pronoun
- technical CVs should be understandable by a non-technical person who has only the person specification in front of them
- pare down the detail to the bare minimum. Avoid flowery and over-wordy sentences.

8 CHRONOLOGICAL CVs

A chronological CV format is one where your work history, qualifications, etc. are displayed in reverse chronological order. This means that your most recent employment appears first on the CV and it works its way backwards to your first job.

It is a straightforward CV format to write as it is organised in a very logical way. However, depending on your work history and target role, there are other formats that may help you to sell your skills more effectively than a chronological CV. This and each of the following chapters will cover a different CV format. You can choose to present your CV in one or more of these formats depending on which suits you best.

This chapter will help you:

■ understand when to use a chronological CV

■ write your CV in this format.

A chronological CV organises its content according to a historical timeline. Employers like them because they can see very easily what your work history and career progression has been. They can also see any career breaks, the length of each employment and any changes in career path.

If you are looking for a role which is a natural progression given your career to date, then the chronological CV format will be appropriate and will highlight your suitability for the role, for example a conference assistant who is looking for a similar role in the same industry or for the next step. Under the most recent employment it should be possible to demonstrate relevant skills and experience that the employer will be interested in. It is also helpful in highlighting the names of your previous employers. This can be advantageous if they are prestigious brands or competitors of your target employer and therefore likely in themselves to attract interest.

However, if your last employment(s) have not been directly relevant to the role you are applying for, then a chronological CV will do you no favours. It will instead raise questions about why you are applying. Equally, if you have had several jobs, gaps between jobs or career breaks, then this CV format could make what is a very legitimate work history look irregular and troublesome. In this case, you would be advised to look at one of the other CV formats, such as a functional CV, which is covered in the next chapter.

Let's look at how you would write a chronological CV using all of the information you have gathered when doing the activities in this book.

PROS AND CONS OF CHRONOLOGICAL CVs

Advantages of a chronological CV

- A chronological format is liked by most employers.

- It is a clear and simple format.

- It is easy to chart your career progression, e.g. promotions or growing specialisation.

- It is more in line with application forms with experience, dates, employment history laid out in a straightforward manner.

Disadvantages of a chronological CV

- A chronological CV will show up any inconsistencies or variations in your career path.

- It can reveal unimportant or inconsequential jobs.

- It can reveal periods of unemployment or brief job tenure.

- It may emphasise your lack of wider experience if you have stayed in one job for a long time.

Template for a chronological CV

Name

Address
Tel:
Email:
Date of birth (optional):

Career profile
(use or adapt the career profile you wrote in Activity 13)
Describe yourself using the same or a similar title to the job you are applying for and give details of your experience in the sector. Follow with a few lines (approximately three to five) which summarise what you have to offer in relation to the job, e.g. key skills and experience. Include a mix of technical, professional and softer skills. Include prestigious brand names, awards, etc. Your profile is the most important part of your CV and it should encourage a prospective employer to read further.

Career history
(use material from Activity 1 on information gathering and Activity 12 for your research on matching you to the role)
- Most recent job title • Organisation • Date (year to year)
- Write a brief description: one to two sentences on the company, its size, products, location, structure (Activity 1).
- Describe your key achievements in your last post, bearing in mind the requirements for the job you are applying for. Quantify those achievements – what difference did it make to the organisation? (Activity 5).
- Do not write your job description here – cherry-pick skills and duties and personal qualities relevant to the role being sought.

Previous job title	Organisation	Date
Previous job title	Organisation	Date
Previous job title	Organisation	Date
Previous job title	Organisation	Date

Go back 10–15 years or more if your job previous to this still has relevance to the job for which you are applying. You can give fewer details the further back you go. Try not to repeat yourself. If you are in danger of doing this, a functional CV may be more appropriate.

If you need to talk about a period where you had several jobs but do not wish to go into specifics you could group them together as 'a variety of roles, including Project Manager, Team Leader, Team Coordinator, which enabled the development of my …'.

Qualifications and training

- List relevant professional qualifications/memberships first, e.g. Trained NVQ Assessor.
- Higher academic qualifications should be listed before others unless lower qualifications are of more immediate relevance.
- School qualifications do not need to be included on the CV where you have higher qualifications.
- Training can be a separate heading. Do not list all training courses but do include those that may have a direct benefit on new employers, e.g. first aid, project management. Remember training does not have to take place in a classroom to have value, e.g. distance learning, e-learning.

Additional information

- This section can be used to include any information that will show you in a good light as a candidate.
- You might like to include any voluntary work that you do, e.g. school governor.
- You can also include language skills, clean driving licence, inventions, achievements outside work.

Interests

This is optional, but can be useful if you have limited work experience and want to give the employer more of a sense about what you are like as a person. Also if you are more 'mature' in years, you can use this section to show that you are fit, energetic and up to date.

The CV should be no more than two pages long unless you need to include lists of publications or research.

CV 1: Chronological CV

Malcolm Mason

Address: 1 Parkgate Road, Fensworth LB1 XYZ
Tel: 01234 555 666
Mobile: 0777 777 666
E-mail: mm@hotmail.co.uk

Career profile

Commercial manager and CIMA qualified accountant, with over 10 years' experience of working within health sector organisations undergoing merger and acquisition. Track record of adding significant value to organisations as a result of rigorous analysis, creative problem-solving and identifying lucrative business opportunities which would otherwise have been missed.

Employment history

Regional Commercial Manager   • Cortins Healthcare Ltd   • 2006 to date
Responsible for financial performance of 10 hospitals with combined turnover of £65 million for Cortins Healthcare Ltd, one of the largest private healthcare providers in the UK.

- Met service delivery targets and budget for all the hospitals under my remit.
- Identified Lady Godwin Hospital as a key target acquisition and as a key member of the bid team, succeeded in acquiring it for £2 million less than requested purchase price.
- Negotiated and agreed fees with hospital consultants. This was a sensitive issue that was crucial to the continued effectiveness and profitability of the organisation.
- Devised strategic plan for continued growth based on in-depth bench-marking exercise, which was adopted by the Board.
- Improved the user-friendliness of the financial information available to department heads and supported managers in developing action plans.
- Negotiated new service level agreement with cleaning company which addressed service shortfalls and provided ongoing monitoring to ensure service standards.

Business Analyst   • Koppen Insurance   • 2001–2005
Koppen Insurance is an international insurance company with a turnover of £300 million, providing diverse insurance products. My role was to grow the financial performance of the new health insurance segment of the business.

- Wrote strategic plan for expansion into private healthcare market, which was approved by the Board and subsequently brought in over £10 million profit into the company within the first year.
- Handled the selling of the unprofitable investment business, preparing all due diligence paperwork, TUPE (Transfer of Undertakings (Protection of Employment) Regulations) transfer, etc.

M Mason 1/2

- Trained new departmental heads in financial management and organisational financial processes.
- Led cross-organisational working group to review service delivery resulting in implementation of several recommendations including re-contracting with NHS providers.

Management Accountant • RST Group • 1997–2001

Responsible for financial accounting processes for the rapidly expanding RST Group. They grew from £10 million revenues to £65 million in the 4 years I was with them.

- Integrated over 10 new corporate acquisitions into RST's financial processes.
- Trained and briefed staff in financial operating procedures.
- Worked closely with managers to set realistic budgets and delivery targets built on well-researched projections.
- Involved in financial accounting for all start ups, acquisitions, extensions, new builds, conversions and product development strategies of the new business growth team.
- Prepared and presented business cases and investment appraisals to the investment committee which led to the development of two brand new services, one of which has since become responsible for over 20% of total revenue.
- Revised internal audit procedures and conducted regular internal audits.

Financial Consultant • Jones Consulting • 1994–1997

Worked for Jones Consulting on several financial projects within the healthcare sector.

- Conducted financial review and assisted in strategy formulation for several NHS primary care trusts.
- Worked in compliance roles on several projects, including blue-chip companies such as DEF and GHI.

Qualifications

CIMA qualified   (first-time pass)
BSc Applied Physics (2:i)   Smalltown University

IT skills

Advanced user of Excel, Pegasus, Aggresso, Microsoft Office, SQL

M Mason 2/2

IN A NUTSHELL

Use a chronological CV when:

- last few roles/employers are directly relevant to job being sought
- you have been promoted and/or been given additional responsibilities throughout your career
- you can demonstrate steady employment and few employment gaps
- you can use well-known companies or prestigious brands to show your calibre.

Don't use a chronological CV when:

- seeking to downplay any career breaks or gaps between employment
- employment includes several short-term jobs which could look like job-hopping
- you want to change career direction from previous career history
- your responsibilities have decreased in the course of your career, e.g. demotions.

9 FUNCTIONAL CVs

A functional CV format offers a highly flexible way of presenting your career history. Unlike a chronological CV, it is not constrained by time structure but is organised around what is going to sell you most effectively to your target employer.

This chapter will help you:

- understand what a functional CV is and when to use it

- write your CV in a functional format.

A functional CV format will enable you to highlight in the first page of your CV the skills and experience you have that are of most relevance to the employer. This can include paid and unpaid work, transferable skills, qualifications or any other additional information which will demonstrate your suitability.

This is a particular advantage if you know you have the skills and experience to do the job, but your current or past employment has been in an unrelated role. Where an employer has detailed specific competencies that are required, you can also use these competencies as headings and provide examples with accompanying evidence.

You can select your headings and order them according to how they will sell you best. Some examples of those you can use are:

- career profile
- career history
- work experience
- key achievements
- responsibilities
- key skills
- key competencies
- education
- qualifications
- training
- innovations
- publication
- additional information
- hobbies/interests
- project experience
- IT skills
- specialist knowledge
- positions of responsibility.

Depending on your experience and the job in question, it may make sense to prioritise some areas rather than others. For example, for jobs in the higher education or research sector, it makes sense to put your educational details first and then include headings for any publications, research, conference speaking events and continuous professional development activities, etc. If you are selling yourself as an IT technical expert, you should specify your technical skills and knowledge up-front.

PROS AND CONS OF FUNCTIONAL CVs

Advantages of the functional CV

- It prioritises the areas of most relevance to the employer.

- You can combine skills and experience used in different jobs to strengthen what could otherwise come across as rather thin experience.

- You can use paid and unpaid work experience to support your application.

- You can omit or downplay any work history that could be seen as a distraction.

- Employment gaps or lots of short-term jobs are not as noticeable as in a chronological CV.

- It allows you to show your transferable skills, which is essential if you are seeking to change career direction or are a less than obvious candidate.

Disadvantages of the functional CV

- Employers are slightly more suspicious of this format given its usefulness in hiding things that the candidate would rather the employer didn't know.

- You will still need to supply the detail of employment dates, qualifications, etc. because the employer will want verification of whom you worked for and when.

- It can sometimes be unclear about the skills you gained from a particular job or experience.

- If you have had good career progression in an appropriate field, a functional CV will not show this to as good an advantage as the chronological CV.

- It can be tricky to get the balance of information right and not make the CV too long.

Chronological detail regarding your employment history is generally relegated to the second page. This means that any gaps in employment, unconnected jobs, etc. are downplayed as you will hopefully have persuaded the employer on the first page that you are suitable for shortlisting.

If you feel that the functional format is a good format for your CV then you can follow the template provided here and use the two sample CVs as a guide.

Template for a functional CV

Name

Address
Tel:
Email:
Date of birth (optional):

Profile
(use or adapt profile written in Activity 13)
Describe yourself using the same or a similar title to the job you are applying for and give details of your experience in the sector. Follow with a few sentences (approximately three to five) that summarise what you have to offer to the job, e.g. key skills and experience. Your profile is the most important part of your CV and should encourage a prospective employer to read further.

Key skills and experience/key achievements or other relevant heading
(use research from Activity 12 on matching you to the role)
- From reading the advertisement or person specification for the job, show directly how you meet the selection criteria, choosing examples of how you demonstrate the competencies required.
- Put the information in bullet points, putting those most relevant to the job you are applying for at the top.
- Think of the skills you have developed from different jobs and even from activities outside work that show the competencies the employer is looking for.
- You can also include sub-headings that match the selection criteria, e.g. financial management, training, etc.
- Include a mix of technical, professional and interpersonal skills.
- Include memberships or affiliations as appropriate.
- For key achievements, use the information you gained from Activities 4 and 5 in Chapter 3 to pick out two or three particular achievements that show your capabilities for the role, e.g. if the employer wants organisational skills, choose an example that shows this off to good effect.
- Quantify those achievements, e.g. increased sales by 30% over 2 months.
- This section will probably take up most of the first page.

Career summary
Most recent job title	Organisation	year to year
Previous job title	Organisation	year to year
Previous job title	Organisation	year to year

You can summarise your jobs or put a couple of lines about key responsibilities under each one. If you need to include a period where you had several jobs but do not wish to go into specifics you could group them together, e.g. '1995–1999, worked in a variety of office-based roles including Personal Secretary, Corporate Secretary, Team Coordinator, which helped me develop my administrative skills and my IT capabilities.'

Qualifications and training

- If qualification is highly relevant include it in the career profile or on the first page. Otherwise list relevant professional qualifications/memberships first, e.g. Trained NVQ Assessor.
- Higher academic qualifications should be listed before others unless lower qualifications are of more immediate relevance.
- School qualifications do not need to be included on the CV where you have higher qualifications.
- Do not list all training courses but do include those that may have a direct benefit on new employers, e.g. first aid, project management.
- Remember training does not have to take place in a classroom to have value, e.g. distance learning, e-learning.

Other information

This may include any other relevant information, e.g. clean driving licence, languages, and any other piece of information which is significant.

Interests

This is optional. Three or four are usually sufficient but do think about whether you would be happy to talk about them and what they say about you. Make sure that they genuinely are your interests.

The CV should be no more than two pages long unless you need to include lists of publications or research.

CV 2: Functional CV (for a candidate with a career gap)

Nita Choudry

58 Oak Avenue, Northport SS5 900
Mobile.: 07777 777555
Email: nc@hotmail.com

Travel manager with 15 years' experience of helping individual and corporate clients with their international travel requirements. Proven ability to bring in new customers as a result of excellent business development skills. Noted for building trusted relationships with both corporate and individual customers, resulting in a high degree of repeat business.

Key skills and experience
- BTEC National Diploma in Travel and Tourism.
- Highly experienced in advising on leisure holidays and efficiently organising arrangements.
- Knowledgeable about visa requirements, travel documents, health protection.
- Excellent crisis management skills including helping travellers experiencing problems such as sickness, loss of documents, accidents.
- Familiar with most travel database software and systems used by external agents such as airlines.
- Management of several corporate accounts where travel arrangements often need to be arranged or re-arranged at very short notice.
- Client evaluations are consistently good with frequent comments on my helpfulness, knowledge and organisational skills.
- Widely travelled all over the world and language skills include French and Spanish.

Employment history
Travel Manager   • Conway Travel   • 2006–2008
Conway Travel is an ABTA (The Travel Association)-registered independent travel agency, with a team of three providing leisure and business travel services.
- Responsible for providing full travel advisory and organisation services to diverse customer base.
- Won new corporate accounts worth £50,000 per year as a result of proactive networking for the business.
- Management responsibilities include supervision of staff, office facilities, health and safety and financial audits to promote high-quality standards.
- Key liaison with travel partners, including airlines and hotels, to manage bookings and schedules and relationships.
- Undertook familiarisation visits to new destinations in the Far East and Africa to gain information on issues and amenities of interest to consumers.

- Actively marketed weekend breaks to new younger market that is now bringing in an additional £500,000 per year.
- Organised incentives, bonus schemes and competitions that helped grow revenue by on average of 10% per year.

Travel Manager • Getaway Travel • 1997–2003
Getaway Travel is an ABTA-registered independent travel agency specialising in holidays for private individuals.
- Advised and arranged package, fly-drive and specialist holidays as well as organising more bespoke packages.
- Promoted and marketed the business to 'niche' markets including activity holidays such as golf, cooking and yoga. This brought in an additional £100,000.
- Managed £100,000 budget and maintained all financial records.
- Recruited and trained two new members of staff.

Travel Assistant • Ultimate Holiday Company • 1994–1996
Ultimate Holiday Company is the market leader in leisure travel and I was fortunate to undertake all of my training while working for it. I received an excellent grounding in the operations of a large-scale commercial travel agency.
- Organising travel arrangements for leisure customers.
- Chasing up and checking tickets, schedules, documentation requirements.
- In-putting customer information on computers and producing print-outs.
- Producing itineraries for customers requiring more tailored packages.
- Researching costings to make sure proposals were within budget.

Education and training
- BTEC National Diploma in Travel and Tourism
- Four GCSEs including English and Maths
- In-house customer service training
- IT skills including database software, Word and Excel

Interests
- Travel, learning Italian, aerobics

N Choudry 2/2

CV 3: Functional CV (candidate who has taken a career detour)

Gillian Knight

38 Coniferous Drive, Lampshire HM1 7RR

Mobile: 07983 999 9999

Email: gk@googlemail.com

CIPD-qualified training officer with 8 years of experience working in the public sector, helping individuals to develop their knowledge and capabilities. Able to work with people at all levels, including senior management teams and junior staff in order to help them achieve learning outcomes. Experienced in organising a wide range of workshops, coaching interventions and e-learning resources.

Training administration

- Managed pensions roadshow that reached over 5,000 employees at 20 regional centres to raise employee awareness about their pension rights.
- Organised attendance at annual sales conference for approximately 100 staff including speaker invitations, attendance lists, workshop schedules, catering and accommodation as well as all programme materials.
- Responsible for ensuring the accurate and timely input of training and development information on the in-house database.
- Produced statistical reports on training activities undertaken throughout the year as the basis for future planning.
- Collated evaluation reports from training and produced summary reports.
- Monitored and arranged the processing of invoices from external training providers.

Assessing training needs

- Experienced in advising managers and staff on training needs and solutions both in-house and externally.
- As a result of staff feedback, initiated and managed the development of in-house learning resources including online materials for self-directed learning.
- Conducted full training review of induction programme making several changes to the existing programme. This resulted in significant improvements in the feedback from participants.
- Liaised with IT department and IT users to determine IT training priorities for year ahead.
- Experienced in identifying and briefing potential training suppliers for courses as varied as appraisal training, compliance and sales.

Coaching

- Trained as an internal career coach as a result of attending in-house career coaching skills programme.
- Mentor for member of the graduate talent programme.
- Responsible for informal coaching and induction of junior staff new to the HR department.

Employment history

Health and Safety Officer	XYZ Government Agency	2004–2008
Training Officer	King George University	2000–2004

Qualifications

Certificate in Training Practice	Distance Learning	2003
BA (Hons) in American Studies (2:ii)	Lincoln University	1997–2000

Training

Day coaching course	Negotiation skills
Appraisal training	Health and safety risk assessment
Managing conflict	Advanced Word

Additional Information

- Excellent IT skills including advanced user of Word, Excel and PowerPoint
- Substantial reading on self-development
- Mentor for a community youth project

G Knight 2/2

IN A NUTSHELL

Functional CVs can be a highly effective way of demonstrating your suitability for a particular role or employer, particularly when you may not be an obvious candidate.

Use when:
- you need extra versatility in the structure of your CV
- last few roles/employers are not as relevant to the job being sought
- your career path has been more haphazard than steady progression
- your employment looks inconsistent, with gaps or lots of short-term roles and you want to play down any work history that could be seen as distraction
- changing career direction to display your transferable skills
- you want a direct way to show the employer how you meet their competency requirements by choosing particular headings in your CV
- you have worked for one employer for most of your career and you want to demonstrate your versatility on the first page rather than emphasise your limited wider experience
- you want to use paid and unpaid work experience to support your application.

Don't use when:
- applying for a role that is directly compatible with your previous roles
- you can show a history of career progression within related roles.

10 ONE-PAGE CVs

Normally your CV should be no longer than two pages long, or occasionally three if you are an academic and need to include details of publications, etc. However, there are occasions in which a one-page CV is required and indeed desirable to send.

This chapter will help you:

- understand when you may want to use a one-page CV

- write your CV in this format.

First a warning: do not send a one-page CV as part of an application for an advertised job unless you have been specifically requested to do so. The two-page format is the default standard.

However, there are particular instances when a one-page CV can be very effective. Most commonly they are used as a 'teaser' advertisement to gain interest or a meeting without giving too much away in the first instance.

Following your research on potential employers in Part 2 of this book, you might use it to send speculatively to an employer you are interested in working for. By carefully cherry-picking certain key skills, knowledge or achievements, which you know will benefit an organisation, you can gain interest and obtain meetings with your target employer.

The other advantage of this CV format is that you don't necessarily need to include your past employment details. You can refer to these indirectly such as '5 years' working as key account manager for well-known household brand'. This can be useful if the details of your employment history are either not helpful or if confidentiality is important. If you are approaching a competitor, you may want to be discreet.

You might also devise a one-page CV if you are self-employed or if your company supplies potential customers with career background on their staff as part of the company's sales

PROS AND CONS OF ONE-PAGE CVs

Advantages of a one-page CV

- It is quick and easy for employer to read.

- It has the ability to be highly selective in information included.

- It can hide details of current employer if still working for them.

- It is effective if making speculative approaches to potential employers, as it can be used to gain interest without giving too much information away.

- It can be used by your current employer to market their services to potential customers.

- If you are self-employed, you can use this format to show your credentials.

- It is appropriate for online forums such as social-networking websites.

Disadvantages of a one-page CV

- It is unsuitable for applying for advertised vacancies.

- It is unsuitable for applying to agencies.

- The balance of information can be tricky to get right.

- Any claims made still need to be substantiated.

pitch. This is particularly relevant for professional service providers, consultancies or any other enterprise where the individual's expertise is a key factor in winning new customers to the company, e.g. training specialist.

Here is a template and specimen CV which you can use as a guide to write your own CV in this format.

Template for a one-page CV

Name

Address (optional)
Tel/Mobile:
Email:

Profile (optional)
Describe yourself in terms of your experience and specialisms. You could include key brand names, organisations worked with or impressive projects.

Key skills and experience or key achievements
* Focus on activities that you have undertaken and that have added value to the organisation, e.g. increased profitability, efficiency, quality.
* Quantify all achievements: use numbers, percentage points, budget size, etc.
* Relate all skills and experience directly to customer's/employer's anticipated needs

Career history
Present this in summary form, for example:
* 2002–2008: Training Consultant, Albin Training Consultancy
* 2000–2002: Training Director, The Shires Training Consultants
* 1995–2000: Training Manager, Train to Train
Alternatively your career history can be written in full sentences without naming organisations, e.g. 5 years' experience of working with organisations as diverse as high-street banks, large-scale accountancy practices and insurance companies, as a management development specialist.

Education/training
Give your highest qualifications and only relevant training.

Affiliations, professional memberships
Include any details that enhance your professional status and/or are prestigious in themselves.

CV 4: One-page CV

Louis Alexander

Mobile: 07777 555 555
Email: lm@hotmail.com

Career profile

Business transformation specialist with over 10 years' experience of working on projects including culture change, work redesign and technological innovations. Highly experienced in projects requiring process mapping/review, streamlining and re-engineering. MBA qualified.

Key consultancy skills

Blueprint Facilitation	Project Health Check
Leading Business Change	Stakeholder Management and Communications
Process Design	Event Planning and Coordination
KPI Strategy	IT strategy
Hypothesis creation	Focus interviews

Employment history

- 3 years' experience as Business Transformation Consultant with international specialist change consultancy.
- 6 years' experience as Business Analyst with one of the big four professional services firms.
- 5 years' experience as Business Solutions Consultant at one of the UK's largest retailers.

Examples of key projects

- **Distributor of office equipment**: Drove a change management programme to resolve key business issues through root-cause analysis and process improvements. Branch net profitability was improved in excess of £500,000 per year and green light given for roll out of the programme throughout the organisation.
- **Local authority**: Led a joint client team in scoping a strategic initiative to improve the effectiveness of customer contacts, while reducing costs. Project evaluated to have improved experience for more than 80% of the customers.
- **International retailer**: Led a critical piece of work to define the business implementation approach for a technology upgrade, supporting over 50 business teams across Europe, Middle East and Africa to capture additional business worth a projected £50 million.

Education

MBASt	James Management College	2001–2005
BSc (Hons) Geography	Edmonds University	1990–1993

IN A NUTSHELL

Use a one-page CV when:

- you are self-employed, to use alongside other company marketing material
- it is required by your own organisation as information for their customers
- you wish to upload your CV to a social networking website
- it is specifically requested by an organisation
- writing a speculative letter to an employer and attaching a CV.

Don't use when:

- you are applying for jobs advertised by an employer or agency as they will expect a chronological or functional CV
- you have good career progression in a related field
- you cannot sprinkle brand names, prestigious companies, projects or substantial money-making achievements in the CV to give it weight.

11 DEVELOPING YOUR OWN CV WEBSITE

It is now relatively easy to set up a website at low cost and for some candidates, particularly for freelancers and those who work in creative fields, it has become essential.

This chapter will help you:

- understand what a CV website is and whether you should have one

- know what to include on the website.

f you have a portfolio of work that prospective employers would find helpful to view, then consider creating your own website. You can use it to display all of your relevant information and background with examples of your work and testimonials from satisfied clients or employers. This approach is highly suitable for individuals in the following and similar fields:

- website developers
- designers
- journalists
- artists
- performers
- film-makers
- freelance employees, e.g. coaches

The links to the website can be included within a traditional CV that you send as normal to an employer or to a recruitment website. You can also include it on business cards. If you email companies directly with a covering email and the link to your website within the body of the email, then you may need to check that they received the email as spam filters can be sensitive to links.

PROS AND CONS OF HAVING YOUR OWN CV WEBSITE

Advantages

- It can replace physically carrying around a portfolio of your work (most of the time).

- There is now an expectation that if you are a creative professional, e.g. a designer, you will have a website with examples of your work.

- There are no limits on space or the type of material you can include.

- You can use photos, video, graphics, sound, links, etc.

- You have the chance to use your creativity in the design of the website, which in itself can impress your target audience as much as the content.

Disadvantages

- It requires financial investment.

- Developing the website can take from weeks to months.

- It needs maintenance – a website where links don't work or the content is not displayed correctly can lose you business.

- It needs regular updating.

- Many roles will still need a conventional CV format.

How to build your own website

If you are interested in setting up your own website , there is a wealth of information available on the internet on how to do this. Simply search on 'how to set up your own website' in your preferred search engine.

The basic steps you will need to take are:

1. Choose a domain name, which will be your website name. It's like choosing a company name in that, first, you need to make sure it's available, and, second, you have to pay to register it. You can find domain name companies by searching on the web.
2. You will need a web host to host your website on the internet, for which another fee is payable, usually annually.
3. Design your website. This will depend on your ambitions, your capabilities and your budget. You can use website templates that you can customise. You can build it from scratch using specialist software if you are capable, or you can get someone else to design it for you. If you are thinking of using a professional, be aware that the costs could range from a few hundred pounds to several thousand for more complex projects.

What to include on your website

If you are using this website to obtain your next role or engagement, then it needs to pay as much attention as a regular CV to your key selling points, and what you think the target audience is looking for. The visual presentation may be more sophisticated, but there is still no margin for error. Poor layout, spelling mistakes, etc. will not be forgiven.

The website should include:

- your name
- how to contact you
- your credentials, e.g. technical skills, relevant qualifications, education
- what you can offer (do the sales pitch!)
- information to impress, e.g. exhibitions, prestige projects, well-known customers
- relevant work history (dates optional)
- photo of you, if you are a performer or you work in an area where a personal relationship is important, e.g. image consultant. Make sure the photo shows you in your professional capacity
- photos of your work (if artist, designer)

- video or sound clips if appropriate
- articles written by you or about you
- quotes, testimonials, glowing reviews or case studies.

A website also gives you the chance to express more personal information, perhaps about your approach to your work, e.g. 'My aim is to surprise and delight my clients with highly innovative design solutions that combine practicality and a sense of fun'.

However, resist the temptation to include irrelevant personal information, e.g. old family photos, early history unless it is directly of relevance. Keep it strictly professional. The audience want to know what you can do for them, not what your favourite bands are.

Overleaf is an example of a website for a web designer. You can find many more examples by typing in 'online portfolio CV' into your preferred internet search engine. It is extremely useful to see what others have developed and what you think works and what doesn't. You can then start to devise your own.

IN A NUTSHELL

- if you normally supply a portfolio of work to customers or potential employers, you should also have your own website.
- remember this is a sales pitch, so focus on what you want to sell and what your target audience wants.
- do not include irrelevant personal information – keep it business-like.
- ensure site is maintained and updated.
- be realistic on budget and stick to it as it is very easy to overspend.
- visually it must look attractive and be error-free.
- ensure it is easy to contact you.
- include link to website either within regular CV or send link separately by email or include on business card.

A web designer's website

_MILLSYinc.

_Elliot Mills
_020 555 555
_em@yahoo.co.uk

_Download CV

_Client List

Gnomes Garden Industries
All-Year-Round Organic Vegetables
St Augustus Horticultural Society
Japanese Koi Fish
'Health Is Wealth' Lifestyle Magazines
Barrington Spa
The Interior Design Company
Just Gorgeous Ornaments
Wood Garden Centres
Garden Wall Art
C&A Landscaping
Greg Dymon Personal Training

Click on a client to show
more work

_Contact me

Name

Email

Query

Submit

MY BACKGROUND

My name is Elliot Mills and this is my portfolio of website and
design work. I am a freelancer so I'm always interested in new
projects. I have 5 years experience of website design work
helping clients within the aspirational lifestyle sector to develop a
customer-friendly, visually pleasing, professional and trouble-free
website.

TECHNICAL SKILLS

Code includes xHtml, JavaScript, CSS, Action script versions 4, 5,
ASP and VB and PHP, Perl. Good understanding of SQL database.
Programmes include Photoshop, Image Ready, Illustrator,
Dreamweaver, Flash, After Effects, Premiere, InDesign and Quark.
Mac OSX and Windows 2000/XP platforms.

CURRENT WEBSITES

www.gnomesgi.com
www.candalandscapes.co.uk
www.ayrorganic.com
www.staugustus.horticulture.co.uk
www.jkfish.com

www.interiordesign.com
www.barringtonspa.co.uk
www.justgorgeous.org.uk
www.woodgardens.com
www.gregdymonpt.com

I take the time to really understand what you are looking for and
will always provide you with a range of ideas from which you can
choose. I have a real creative flair and the ingenuity to provide
highly impressive websites which are inspiring, functional yet also
low maintenance.

TESTIMONIALS

"We were delighted with our site. Elliot completed it in record time
and he really got the essence of how we wanted the site to work.
We were very pleased!" S. Moon ABC Ltd

"As complete beginners to the internet, Elliot helped us to
understand our options and make great choices regarding the
design and functionality of our site. He also kept costs within the
budget we had set. We would highly recommend him!"
M. Malone RST UK

12 HOW TO MAKE YOUR CV LOOK GOOD

Employers will judge your professionalism not only by the content of your CV but also by the standard of its presentation.

This chapter will help you to:

- produce a CV that is visually attractive as well as functional

- know the etiquette for sending your CV by post

- decide whether to send a photo

- quality check your CV so that it is error free.

A nicely presented CV says to the recruiter that you have taken care in your application, and therefore you are likely to:

- want the job because you have clearly made an effort
- have good quality standards because of your attention to detail
- act as a good representative for the company because you understand how to make a good impression.

Your CV must be produced using a computer – even if the role for which you are applying does not require IT skills. A CV or covering letter that is hand-written, or which shows poor IT skills, will make you look very old-fashioned and is almost certainly going to end up on the reject pile.

The relative ease with which documents can be produced and amended electronically also means that there are high expectations regarding the aesthetics of the CV and a low tolerance of mistakes.

If you don't have strong IT skills, there are several ways to improve and this is a very worthwhile investment. Check out www.learndirect.co.uk for more information on online programmes and also courses at your local college. IT facilities can also be found at libraries and internet cafés.

However, if you are really struggling with the IT demands of writing a CV, then ask someone else if they can type it for you as a favour, or pay to have it done professionally through a local secretarial service or CV service. Then, go and get yourself on a course.

Making your CV look attractive

The following guidelines are designed to help you lay out your CV in a way that reinforces the highly professional image you are trying to convey.

BEAUTIFY YOUR CV

- **Compatibility:** formatting options such as columns, shading, boxes, etc. may look nice, but they could interfere with the recruiter's software package. Avoid these formatting options, unless you have checked that the format will be compatible.

- **Font size:** choose one font to use throughout. Arial or Times New Roman 10–12 pt always work well.

- **Margins:** use margins of at least 2.5cm on either side and on the top and bottom of the page.

- **Headings:** use a consistent style for headings, either bold, all capitals and/or slightly bigger font. Underlining looks messy and can confuse some recruitment and scanning software.

- **Bullet points:** use a standard bullet point formats as unusual symbols can confuse software.

- **Punctuation:** be consistent in the use of full stops at the end of bullet points and/or paragraphs.

- **Alignment:** make sure all headings, para-graphs, etc. are in line with each other.

- **Justification:** text looks better if it is not justified as this can leave odd spacing in the copy.

- **White space:** make sure that around headings and paragraphs of text there is plenty of white space to make it look aesthetically pleasing. If you are struggling to get your information into two pages, it is better to edit and remove text rather than pack it in too tightly so it looks cramped.

- **Colour:** your CV will be printed out and photocopied in black and white so make sure it works well in monochrome format.

- **Length:** aim for a CV that is no longer than two A4 pages. The only exception are academics who need to list their publications, presentations, etc..

- **Footers:** include your name and the page number in the footer of each page in case they get muddled once printed out.

- **Creatives:** if you are in a creative profession, you may want to demonstrate your design abilities within your CV. Do this in a PDF format but make sure that the recipient can read it, as photos or Jpegs may be blocked by spam filters.

The basic principles of CV writing apply no matter what your personal situation. Research the job, demonstrate you have what they are looking for and then organise the information on the page in an attractive and professional manner.

This chapter offers additional tips for where organising and presenting the content presents its own challenges.

CVs for graduates and school-leavers

Looking for your first 'proper' job is exciting and daunting. How do you convince an employer you are a great person to hire, when you have limited work experience to draw on?

Well, everyone has to start somewhere. What employers are looking for in their young staff is potential: the capacity to learn, the motivation to work hard and the ability to get on with people. They also want to see that you have thought about why you are suitable for the role and that you genuinely want to do it.

So, let's look at how your CV can help convince them that you have got what it takes.

Career objective/career profile

If you are using your CV for a specific role, include a career objective that states you are looking exactly for that role. For example, a graduate with experience of working Saturdays with an electrical retail store might apply for a sales-type role with this career profile:

'Business graduate experienced in retail sales and customer service environments. Used to advising customers on a range of complex technical products, processing sales and helping with merchandising. Regularly earned bonuses as a result of meeting personal and team targets. Looking for a position where I can further my interest in sales and business development.'

However, if they wanted to apply for an accountancy role then they could try:

'Business graduate seeking trainee accountancy role to further my interest in the financial aspects of running a business. Used to dealing with cost calculations, payment processes and following strict financial procedures as a result of my experience working for large electrical retailer.'

Academic studies

You may want to put this as one of your first headings so that they can see you are a new job-hunter.

Include details about the components of your course only if it is directly relevant to the job sought, e.g. you have a marketing degree and are applying for a marketing-related role or your course has given you an awareness of the organisation's industry or product.

You may want to highlight under your studies any involvement in the following highly transferable skills:

- data analysis, interpreting statistical information
- IT skills
- team-working, group project work
- communication and presentation skills
- report writing
- creativity, initiative and design ability.

Employers particularly want good communication skills, so this is an area to emphasise throughout your CV.

If your courses were completed abroad indicate the level to which they are equivalent, e.g. Baccalauréat (the A level equivalent). Some graduate entry programmes will require you to have a minimum grade on your degree. This is usually a non-negotiable requirement, and if you don't meet the employer's specific requirements then you might as well not apply. However, if you are intent on working for that particular organisation you can always look to enter via a different route, i.e. direct entry into one of their other jobs.

Relevant experience: young people by definition have less experience so you have to make the most of what you have. You can do this by highlighting prominently on your CV any work experience that is directly related to your target role (paid or unpaid), for example:

- student placements
- temporary jobs within the target field
- relevant voluntary work.

CV 5: Recent graduate CV

Sian Forrester

24 Green Street
Forreston
SV5 ABC
Tel: 0777 555 555

Career profile

Advertising graduate with sound knowledge and work experience within the industry. Undertook placements within an above-the-line advertising agency where I supported staff working on client briefs and assisted the planning team. Sales and customer service skills have been gained from working in a number of different retail environments where I achieved set targets. My ability to build strong relationships was demonstrated in the repeat business I encouraged from high-spending customers. I am looking to combine my advertising background with my sales abilities to work in an account management role with a creative agency.

Education

BSc (Hons) 2:i, Advertising   • Cartell University   • 2005–2008

- Course subjects include: Creative advertising, media, marketing and sales, e-marketing and consumer behaviour, communications psychology.
- Researched and devised our own advertising campaigns which were judged by industry professionals.
- Built own e-commerce website: www.sf.hotmail.com
- Financial management including budget-setting, cost control, forecasting, monitoring, etc.
- Advanced PowerPoint, Word, Excel and Publisher skills.
- Report writing on many advertising related tasks.

1997–2004   • St Augustine High School, Pelham

- 3 A Levels: English (B), Economics (B), French (C)
- 6 GCSEs English Language (A*), Economics (A*), French (A), Mathematics (B*), Chemistry (B*), Geography (C).

S Forrester 1/2

Experience

Placement   • 2007 and 2008   • Deft Advertising Agency

First worked for Deft in 2007 but invited back for 2008. My activities included:

- Helping compile a research summary on a client's competitors for strategy discussion
- Verifying facts for a pitch to a prospective corporate client
- Providing administrative support for the team working on live client briefs including typing up notes and using Excel for contact lists. All work needed to be completed to the highest standards of presentation
- Liaising with the art directors and copy writers regarding the sending of documentation
- Working with the accounts function to understand their process and helping with the client billing records
- Supporting the planning team in organising a direct mail campaign to over 10,000 businesses
- Helping wherever required in the office, including welcoming visitors, refreshments and message-taking.

January 2006 to June 2007   • Amy's Boutique

Worked as sales assistant in this fashionable high-end dress store. This involved:

- Helping the team achieve monthly sales targets
- Keeping the store display immaculate to retain the store's particular image
- Assisting with stock taking to ensure accurate records and identify any items to be put in the annual sales
- Asked for personally by a number of customers who I had advised in the past.

February 2005 to January 2006   • Grant Jason Shoes

Worked as sales assistant in shoe shop. This included:

- Keeping waiting times low by assisting customers quickly and efficiently
- Processing payments for purchases and notifying the manager of any payment issues
- Helping organise the stockroom to make it easier to find required shoes
- Increasing customer spend by recommending shoe accessories
- Assisting with store security to ensure stock was protected from potential theft or damage
- Working to group weekly sales targets.

Additional information

- Editor of the *Student Magazine*
- Run online forum for film buffs
- Mentor to student on my course
- French language skills

S Forrester 2/2

- Conduct performance reviews with eight team members per year plus monthly individual and team meetings. Determine team and individual bonuses against business and personal targets.
- Mentor to two graduate trainees, both of whom are now on the internal fast-track programme.

Training and development

- Identified key competencies and behaviours required from team through conducting in-depth analysis in liaison with training manager and external HR specialist.
- Conducted skills diagnostic for individuals and team as a whole and set targets to bridge areas of gap.
- Organised a series of formal and informal training solutions ranging from classroom-based teaching to coaching, and work shadowing.

Career history

2000 – present   • Service Manager • BRG Holdings

Joined this fast-paced technology organisation as a graduate trainee and was quickly promoted to manager. Current responsibilities include managing team of eight direct reports:

- Improved team productivity by 15% as a result of re-allocation of duties.
- Appointed project team leader on new Customer Service initiative, rolling out key messages through leading workshops, organising training, producing written materials, etc. As a result customer evaluations improved by 25%.
- Key liaison person for new £10 million service level agreement which, although initially unpopular, has weathered the earlier difficulties to deliver substantial cost savings and efficiencies.
- Created partnership agreements on technological contracts with leading players such as Jason White Group and Dales Consultants, which led the way for joint ventures worth £25 million.
- Reduced absence by 20% in my department as a result of tackling and resolving a particularly sensitive health issue that previously no-one had been willing to address.

Education

BA American Studies	Cartell University	1997–2000
CIPD, CPP	Central University	Commencing November 2008

Training

2-day coaching course	Recruitment and Selection	Objective setting
Disciplinary and Grievance	Appraisal Training	Influencing Skills
1st-line Management Course	Managing Absence	Handling conflict

C Gabel 2/2

CVs for people with career gaps

Few people have worked continuously from their first job to retirement and most people will have gaps somewhere in their career for all kinds of reasons including:

- Being dismissed
- Caring for a relative or other dependant
- Ill-health or an accident
- Maternity leave
- Being in prison
- Resigning and then looking for a new role
- Travelling
- Taking some time out for other reasons.

However, employers can be quite suspicious of career gaps and, depending on the length and frequency of the gaps, will want to be reassured that there is no hidden problem.

How do you deal with this?

Date format

Where the gap is only a few months, you can use the month to month or even year to year format for employment dates, e.g. January 2007– March 2008 (for gaps of a few weeks either end) and 2007–2008 (for gaps of a few months). You could even group together a few different past employments, e.g. 2006–2008: During this time, undertook varied administrative roles for organisations such as Jackson Foods and Dales Consultants in the telecommunications and retail sector.

Functional CV format

Use this CV format to highlight on the first page all of your key skills and experience. Put all past employer details and dates on the second page, which will serve to downplay their importance.

Give a positive explanation

If the gaps are still noticeable you may need to give an explanation. It is fine to put down career break for family reasons if you were raising a family or looking after a relative. Equally if you were travelling, studying, or on an interesting adventure, then these are also fine to state.

However, do not put down unemployment or redundancy as a reason for a career gap. Although it may be technically true, unfortunately it does give a negative image of a candidate who has struggled to find a buyer for their skills. Try instead to find some positive way to describe what you were doing at that time. Talk about any voluntary work you were undertaking, studying, writing, helping out with a friend's business, or working with a career coach to decide on your next move. Present an active, positive image of someone who may not have been in paid employment, but who was pursuing activities that added to their employability.

If the reason for the gap is a negative one such as illness or an accident then include this as an explanation on your CV only as a last resort. Any mention of poor health, even if it was a long time ago, will raise concerns over your fitness to work. If you do mention it, phrase the wording to make it clear that whatever medical problem there was, it is now fully resolved, for example 'Unable to work as broke my foot in accident. Now fully recovered.' If there is an on-going health issue that may affect your ability to work, or you are an ex-offender, see Chapter 1 for more information on how to handle these with an employer.

Prove you are ready to work

If you are looking to return to work after a career gap, then you will need to demonstrate to the employer that you have kept your skills fresh during your time away, that you are up to date, up to speed and willing and ready for the challenges of a full working life.

This could include:

- helping run a family/friend's business
- party planning
- reading professional journals
- re-training for a new career direction
- running your own small business
- taking a refresher course in your occupational field, e.g. teaching, nursing
- voluntary committee work
- voluntary work
- work placements.

You will also need good IT skills and so, if you have been away for a while, an IT course should probably be your first port of call. The above examples will all supply good evidence for your CV of your readiness to return to work.

The following CV is an example of someone wishing to return to paid employment following maternity leave. She also wants to change career direction and work in education rather than go back into her original field of market research. She has undertaken voluntary work at her local school to gain relevant experience and to check whether this is something that she enjoys. She has taken advantage of every training course available at the school. She sees the first step of classroom assistant as the means to helping her achieve a transition into the educational field.

CV 7: Returning to work following maternity leave and wanting to change career direction

Pat Jones

1 Gray's Court
Middletown BC5 678
Mobile: 0789 555 555
Email: pjones@gmail.co.uk

Career profile

Classroom assistant with experience of working with children in educational and informal settings at school and in the community. CRB checked and trained in first aid. Have attended workshops on how to deal with children with special needs and used this to good effect while assisting a pupil with mobility challenges. Excellent numeracy and written skills gained from market research background. Strong IT skills. Have great interest and passion in helping children to develop their potential. Looking for a classroom assistant role to pursue this aim. Due to attend classroom assistant training in January 2009.

Relevant skills and experience

- Knowledge and experience of classroom work through working as teacher's helper for Reception and Year 1 at local primary school.
- Assisted teacher in Year 1 in helping to manage particular pupils with challenging behaviour in line with school policy.
- Supported primary school children with their reading and helped in the library, encouraging the children to have fun with books.
- Took care of the younger children in helping them with their lunch and toileting arrangements.
- Supervised the children in the cookery class, helping them learn about healthy eating and make snacks to take home.
- Have attended courses in health and safety, diversity and child protection.
- Involved in running of local toddler group including preparation for an inspection, which was highly complimentary regarding the resources available, the group's organisation and safety standards.
- Highly IT literate, so able to help pupils develop their computer skills and to support teachers with creative use of their electronic whiteboard.
- Ability to communicate effectively to wide range of people developed through previous experience as a market researcher.

P Jones 1/2

Work experience

Classroom helper • Hays School, Gorton • 2008 – present
- Supporting the teacher within the classroom by helping individual children with work activities, e.g. reading.
- Administrative duties, e.g. photocopying, making teachers resources, checking paperwork.
- Assisting a special needs child with mobility challenges to move around the school.
- Provided extra support on school visits to places such as the village library, a farm and the local museum.
- Helping the children look after the school garden, sowing seeds and watering plants.

Career break • 2002–2008
During this time, I was involved in:
- Organising school events (PTA committee member)
- Helping run a voluntary community toddler playgroup that achieved superb feedback following an inspection.
- Administrative work for the family business including typing correspondence, spreadsheets, etc.
- Freelance market research project work.

Market researcher • Jason White Group • 1998–2002
- Devising and leading market research campaigns via customer focus groups, one-to-one interviews and street surveys.
- Designing and evaluating questionnaires to meet the client's objectives.
- Analysing information and producing statistical reports to enable clients to make informed decisions.
- Supervising and inducting other market researchers.
- Ensuring quality control through all aspects of the market research process.

Education and qualifications

BSc Biology (2:i) • University of Greaterhampton • 1993–1996
Three A levels, History (B), Geography (B) Economics (C), and eight. GCSEs, including English and Maths.

IT skills

Excellent Word, Excel and PowerPoint Skills. Also experienced in working with a number of different databases to input data and produce detailed reports.

Interests

Reading, swimming and genealogy.

P Jones 2/2

Technical CVs

When an employer is looking for a candidate with specific technical skills, your first priority is to demonstrate you have the particular expertise they are looking for. Without this, your CV will not be considered. However, given that your CV is most likely to be viewed first by a non-technical person, usually a recruitment agent or HR officer, it also needs to appeal to and be easily understood by a non-technical person. You also need to remember that just as for any other CV, you also need to present an image of a candidate who has all the desirable personality behaviours, for example good communication skills, conscientiousness, etc.

Let's look at how you can achieve the balance between the hard technical skills in your CV and the softer skills.

Keywords

Keywords on your CV are essential if recruiters and employers are to find you on their candidate application database. You therefore need to list all of your technical skills, qualifications and relevant courses for the job. Put these on the first page of your CV and prioritise those that are of most relevance to the employer. Look through job descriptions, advertisements, etc. for a list of common keywords which appear for your target role and make sure they are all included.

Repetition

Be repetitive in regard to the technology, e.g. Java mentioned in several places in the CV confirms that you have a lot of Java experience, as opposed to it just being mentioned once.

Years of experience

Include the number of years of experience you have of a particular technology as a keyword search can be used to prioritise candidates with a specified amount of experience, e.g. more than 5 years' experience.

CV format

A functional CV format may be most helpful as it will prioritise the relevant skills on the first page of your CV. Length of CV is ideally still two pages. However, an experienced developer could have a longer CV as it lists all of the key projects with which they have been involved. IT professionals may also consider hosting their own CV website to show off their technical skills in the construction of the site as well as its content.

Bigger picture

Show your understanding of the bigger business picture and that you do not operate in an 'expert' ivory tower, by including achievements that talk about how your work helped increase organisational efficiency or quality, etc.

Soft skills

Emphasise your communication skills, something that technical people often neglect to mention but which are essential in any job. Include examples of communicating with technical teams and non-technical people, for example external consultants, end users and customers. Technical CVs are often so dry and full of functional detail about programming languages, etc. that they neglect to give a sense of the individual as someone who is easy to work with.

Project work

If you are working in interim or in-house projects, highlight the projects of most relevance to your target employer. Under each project include three to five sentences detailing:

- the company (or the type of company) if confidential
- reasons for hiring you, e.g. employed for my extensive expertise in XYZ
- scope of your project, size, budget, number of users affected, etc.
- the principal challenges or any obstacles faced
- what you did
- the benefit to the company.

Project management/technical management

- Focus on project size, value, number of staff, etc. Include project budget estimating, planning and preparation, requirements gathering and solicitation techniques, monitoring, risk assessment, quality control, etc.
- Demonstrate your ability to quickly build trusted relationships, establishing rapport and respect with business customers and other staff.
- Show your ability to manage and work with diverse teams of people, including actual and virtual teams if appropriate.
- Include examples of handling difficult projects and how you steered them back on course.
- State projects that were completed on schedule, to budget, etc.
- Include any favourable quality evaluations.
- Emphasise people and financial management skills, e.g. budgeting, monitoring finances, recruiting and developing staff, etc.

Starting a career in a technical field

You may have attended your course and obtained your technical qualifications but employers will want to see how you have applied your skills. This is of course more of a challenge when you are just starting your career and your experience is limited. If this is the case, consider offering free or low-cost technical services to family, friends, charitable organisations, etc. If you are a website developer perhaps you could devise one for your local community group, charity or a friend to enable you to build up a portfolio of your work.

In your CV use the career profile/objective statement to focus on your ability to learn quickly, your enthusiasm for this kind of work and your intention to pursue a career in this direction.

The CV example in this section is of a web-developer with three years' professional experience who is looking to specialise in e-commerce. He specifies the technical skills used for each project, and also demonstrates his understanding that his work needs to help his clients make money.

CV 8: Technical CV

Robert Ongwe

1 Canada Street, Greater Morton SL1 345
Mobile: 07777 555 555
Email: rongwe@gmail.co.uk

Career profile

Web-developer with 3 years' experience in developing and maintaining e-commerce websites for international businesses. Able to deliver a customer-friendly internet experience which provides sophisticated back-end management information systems using standard and bespoke packages. Enjoy advising and training non-technical staff on how to maximise the potential of their website. Extensive knowledge and interest in e-commerce marketing, an area in which I wish to specialise further.

Key skills

- Technical skills: MySQL, SQL Server, IIS, UNIX/LINUX, Microsoft Visual SourceSafe
- Languages: PHP, Java, ASP.Net, C#, HTML, DHTML, XML, XSLT, JavaScript, CSS

Education

BSc Computer Science (2:i)　　　　• University of Crawford　　• 2002–2005
Course included: web technology; computer architecture; Java, software systems; algorithms and data structures; advanced database systems; operating systems and networks graphical user interfaces.

Career history

Compuware Consultancy Services　　• July 2006 – present　　• e-Commerce Web-developer
Compuware provides IT consultancy services for organisations ranging from SMEs to multinational corporations.

- Designed and developed bespoke multicurrency e-shop for Bright Greeting Cards using SQL Server and ASP.Net, incorporating payment systems, customer account management, stock control and tracking information. This increased turnover by 45% in the first year.
- Used MySQL to re-vamp payment arrangements for online gaming website using a secure key-based system. Created facility for one-off and subscription payments, loyalty schemes, bonus item codes and special deals for referring a friend. This increased average customer spend by 15% per visit.
- Devised stock control systems and Point of Sale (POS) interfaces using MS SQL Server to improve sales and delivery information for a high-volume retailer. This helped ease distribution log-jams which had previously caused difficulty.

R Ongwe 1/2

- Designed bespoke shopping cart design for RST UK, a high-end fashion retailer using JavaScript. The aim was to complement the products by offering an attractive and unique interactive product browsing experience.
- Advised customers on search engine optimisation, generating reports using Google Analytics and Hitwise. Extensive liaison with SEO specialists to support marketing campaigns through organic campaigns and pay per click.
- Maintenance of several websites using HTML, CSS, PHP and browser-based content management systems to ensure fully functioning at all times.
- Initiated regular tests to benchmark conversion rates and as a result managed to increase click through rate by 10% for five clients within the first month of analysis.
- Have initiated extensive research on SEO, including in-depth reading, attendance at related forums, keeping up to date with latest developments in this field.
- Client evaluations have frequently rated my input to be of a high standard and commented on my helpfulness.

| Maytec Solutions | • June 2005 – June 2006 | • Web-developer |

London-based IT consultancy offering a range of web-based services to corporate clients predominantly in the creative and media field.

- Experienced in the functional testing of both new and existing sites, usability, accessibility, interface and browser capability.
- Providing maintenance and answering queries from customers regarding existing sites and advising on enhancements.
- Designed and developed web-based survey builder using PHP to interactively create and display surveys online.

| Dales Marketing Services | • December 2003–2005 | • Telesales Adviser |

Worked for this company throughout my student course where I was involved in telemarketing on behalf of local businesses.

- Contacting potential customers via cold-calling.
- Working to set targets regarding quantity and quality of telephone calls.
- Keeping accurate records and complying with Data Protection regulations.

Additional information
- Graduate member of British Computing Society.
- Hobbies include cycling, football and singing in a choir.
- My online profile: www.ongwe.com
- Examples of my e-commerce websites: www.xyz; www.def; www.jkl; www.abc; www.ghi; www.mno; www.pqr; www.tuv

R Ongwe 2/2

Creative CVs

If you are applying for a role as a creative professional as a designer or to an organisation that delivers a creative product or service, for example a media company, then be careful of your assumptions about the kind of person you think they are looking to hire. Not all creative roles or organisations are alike. Some will look for high originality, others may prioritise speed and meeting deadlines. You need to know which you should be emphasising on your CV.

The layout of your CV is always being judged. However, for those applying for design roles there is an added challenge. The level of artistic skill, creative thinking and tastefulness that you display in your CV format will be a great influence when it comes to shortlisting.

However, before getting too carried away with the design, always remember that the most important thing on any CV is to demonstrate with examples how you match what the employer is looking for. So make sure the content is written first, before starting to work on the design.

- **Skills and experience:** establish your credibility early on. Prioritise relevant training skills and experience and highlight any required software training or qualifications
- **Enthusiasm:** employers will be looking for a sense of your passion for this type of work, so use lots of positive action words to communicate this. You may want to include how your work extends into your hobbies, e.g. teaching art classes.
- **Gimmicks:** gimmicky CVs can be fun and certainly grab attention but are not always practical. How can you photocopy a CV printed on a T-shirt? Make sure that your CV is readable and usable, otherwise it will end up in the reject pile.
- **Business-focused:** while they may appreciate your original thinking, like any other employer, they will also want to know that you work quickly, cost-effectively and to high-quality standards, so give examples of when you have done this.
- **Rave reviews:** include any examples where your work has been judged favourably by others, e.g. any awards won, commendations, repeat business.
- **Artist statement:** if you are a creative artist, you could also include a short and clear statement of your work and thoughts as an artist. Feel free to use relevant industry terminology as you will most likely be dealing with industry professionals. Statements can include information on the themes of your work, the direction it is heading in, its meaning, etc. This can be tricky to get right, so it's helpful to get feedback from others on whether this is striking the right tone.

Designers

- Design students can create their CVs using a professional publishing package such as Quark or In Design. You can have fun using graphics, logos, photos, columns, shapes, watermarks, colour, etc. Just be careful not to over-design it and remember that if it is printed out, any colour will be irrelevant so make sure that it also looks good in black and white. Pay particular attention to font and typography. Your CV will need to be converted to Adobe PDF if it is to be emailed.

- You can try to create a CV that has a distinctive visual identity, rather like your own personal branding. Use it as a theme that works with your website, business cards, etc. in the same way that you would with a corporate client.
- Including examples of your work can personalise the CV. Label each image and be careful not to overcrowd. Lay these out tastefully and provide a link to other examples of your work on your website. Make sure the images on the CV are appropriate to the vacancy, that is don't include print work if you are going for a digital media role. You may choose not to include any images, and if so the impact of layout and typography becomes more crucial.
- Consider creating your own online CV, where you can include detailed examples of your portfolio. Include the link to the website on your CV.
- Print your CV on high-quality paper. The print finish must be impeccable.

Media CVs

Jobs in the media are desired by many but achieved by relatively few. In order to differentiate yourself from the many, you need to demonstrate that you are a serious candidate with the required technical background and knowledge. Although every role is different, you will also probably need boundless energy, stress tolerance and the ability to work with some fairly demanding personalities.

- Emphasise all courses, training and technical skills you have gained that qualify you for this role.
- Use positive action words throughout to show energy.
- Show how you are passionate about this work, perhaps through hobbies, e.g. running a community drama group or a film club.
- The media is a business that thrives on networking, so include as many well-known names in your CV as you can, to bolster your credibility by association.
- Write an achievement-based CV to present you as a 'go-getter'. Modesty does not work on media CVs.
- Include examples of ideas you generated that worked, problems solved – present yourself as an indispensable person.

Performer CVs

If you are an actor, singer or other performer, you need a very different type of CV.

- Use a one-page CV.
- Specify where your artistic training took place. Other educational qualifications are largely irrelevant unless it was a very prestigious educational establishment.
- Include a photo which has been professionally produced, to accompany your CV. Usually a 10' by 8' head shot in black and white for actors or a colour full-length photo for a presenter.
- State your height, colour of hair, eye colour, playing age and accents you can speak and sing in.
- List your experience by breaking down the productions and directors into film, television and theatre. Specifically name any prestigious directors, co-stars, etc. to build credibility by association.
- Singers should state their voice type and styles, e.g. soprano and musical styles.
- Always provide a professional portfolio with which you can demonstrate your abilities. Ideally this will be via a website where you can post photos, video, reviews.
- Include the name and contact details of your agent.
- Spotlight (www.spotlight.com/artists.html) is the photographic directory of all actors in the UK and is the first place directors look when casting, so your CV should be put in there.

The following CV is an example of a CV for a graphic designer, where the layout is as important as the content. The designer has personalised it with examples of his work but remembered that as in any business, employers are interested in employees who deliver the goods to a high standard and bring in the business.

CV 9: Creative CV for a graphic designer

8 Marsh Lane, Northwoods, SP1 888
0776 777 777
JSmith@email.com

CAREER PROFILE

Graphic designer interested in providing fun, memorable images that get my clients noticed. Skilled in all aspects of print design, logos, posters, leaflets and sales materials; my work combines functionality with a strong brand image that communicates the client's message clearly and distinctively. Many of my clients have been so happy with the work that they have commissioned further work and/or recommended my company to others.

QUALIFICATIONS AND TRAINING

BA (Hons) 2:1 Graphic Design
Grant University 1999–2002

Expert software skills: Illustrator, Photoshop, Quark, InDesign, Macromedia, Adobe, Quark Xpress, Corel

WORK EXPERIENCE

The Graphic Design Company   2005–2008

- Won SE Design award for my work on the Grow Organic account.
- Provided the creative input to the sales pitches that successfully brought over £100,000 worth of business to the company from high-profile clients such as Grant and Thornton, Vista Software Solutions and Global Marketing Group.
- Led design team on production of suite of sales literature for Dales Consultants which involved complete re-branding in line with new corporate mission statement.
- Designed logo and corporate literature for a new legal organisation (Formant and Jones) following merger of two separate companies
- Commissioned by Wright Stationery Ltd. to produce corporate brochure in line with corporate social responsibility guidelines, e.g. recycled paper.
- Created innovative promotional pack for Harris Clothing sales staff using three-dimensional models.
- Devised fun direct-mailing pack for Go for It! advertising campaign.
- Developed advertising campaign for Falstaff Organic Farm for the local paper.
- Created poster advertising campaign for launch of new lifestyle service rolled-out via banners and posters on buses, tube and taxis.

• Created exhibition materials including posters, leaflets, banners, T-shirts for Best Job Recruiters attendance at trade fairs.
Designed business cards, leaflets and advertisements for Inkwell Consultants Ltd.

Elderflower Design   2003–2005

• Quickly promoted to work on larger projects because of the feedback the company received from customers.
• Designed leaflets for Youth Outreach and was then commissioned to produce a whole suite of other marketing materials worth over £50,000.
• Developed sales literature for Shardwell Electronics sales representatives.
• Devised a three-dimensional calendar for promotional use.
• Produced exhibition materials for Shardwell Electronics for prestigious conference event.
• Devised T-shirts for fun run charity event sponsored by The Women's Group.

INTERESTS

Film, art galleries, cycling, scuba-diving, painting

CV advice for managers and executives

A managerial role is generally one which has responsibilities for planning and directing the work of others. They usually work at an operational level in the business, responsible for a particular department or function. If you are applying for managerial-type roles, then in addition to job-specific information there will be some generic skills and competencies that are likely to be required.

Examples of these are outlined below:

■ staff management experience
■ financial management
■ commercial acumen and business awareness
■ strategic planning, conceptualising, forecasting
■ relationship management upwards, downwards, sidewards, externally
■ planning, scheduling and resourcing activities
■ defining and setting targets for team
■ problem-solving, objective decision-making

- self-confidence and stress tolerance
- ability to drive change
- high-level verbal skills, including presentation skills, influencing, negotiating, conflict management
- high-level written skills: presentation of complex information, setting out business sector or job knowledge as appropriate.

An executive has a role which encompasses organisation-wide responsibilities and the strategic side of the business. In addition to the competencies required by managers, an executive will also need to demonstrate in their CV that they have acted on a larger stage, for example:

- strategic planning for the whole organisation rather than just one department
- setting budgets for others rather than just for their own department
- increasing profitability and efficiency for the whole organisation
- external focus to the larger business environment
- setting targets and goals for others.

Executive CVs should therefore focus on achievements and should give examples of activities which:

- increase profitability and efficiency
- introduce and implement change
- demonstrate astute financial management
- help the business grow
- manage adverse conditions
- manage relationships internal and external to organisation
- improve quality of operations under your remit
- research and make informed decisions on complex matters
- produce reports or presentations to support a business case
- set and achieve targets for team, department, or organisation
- specify the size and scope of your responsibilities, e.g. size of budget managed, number of staff.

Here is an example of a director's CV that highlights the professional qualifications required for the job and the input they have made to the success of the organization as a whole.

CV 10: Director's/manager's CV

Jo Chapman

Address: 22 High End Road, Galston AB9 XYZ
Telephone No: 01555 555 555
Mobile: 07755 444 444
Email: jc@yahoo.co.uk

Career profile

Finance Director with 20 years' experience working within the advertising business. Highly experienced in contract negotiation, preparing and winning contracts worth over £15 million in the past 2 years alone. Facilitated a number of strategic changes which improved the financial stability and income potential for the organisation. Used to working in fast-paced environments with high sensitivity to market conditions. Track record of identifying profitable growth opportunities while ensuring very careful risk management.

Career history

Finance Director • J G Howard Advertising Group • 2000–2008
J G Howard is a leading advertising agency with turnover of £100 million and 200 staff. Major clients include blue-chip companies such as Formant and Jones, Dales Consultants and Berkshire Construction Group. Responsible for leading finance team of seven and responsible for another five in the property and legal teams.

- Won Dales Consultants contract worth £15 million in 2007. Responsible for preparing and delivering the financial bid that has opened up a brand new business opportunity within the transport sector with substantial growth potential.
- Project-managed the implementation of the Dales Consultants contract, including organising staff, technology and financial requirements to achieve launch within only 4 months of agreeing the contract.
- Doubled the profit from advertising revenues for major client by negotiating preferred supplier deal on massively advantageous terms.
- Introduced new financial management system to facilitate improved financial modelling capabilities. Linked this with training of finance and operational managers to show how this information could be used at departmental level to improve monitoring of financial performance.
- Identified business opportunity to partner with academic institutions such as universities, which enhanced credibility on certain 'blue-sky' projects.
- Achieved necessary cost-savings of over £2 million in 2006 as a result of difficult market conditions. Redundancies were minimised as a result of careful cost control, natural staff attrition and a recruitment freeze.

- Reworked presentation of our costing proposals to improve transparency and avoid re-negotiations further down the line.
- As Board Director, helped devise and resource organisational strategy to achieve financial robustness, move towards a more diverse client base, and grow the business opportunities within a tight market.

Financial Controller • Wright Stationery Limited • 1995–2000

Reporting to Finance Director and responsible for 10 staff and the operational management of the Finance function.

- Identified business opportunity for York Design to partner with Wright Stationery to achieve cost savings of over £200,000 per annum on resource costs, premises and shared support functions.
- Project-managed the sale of sister company Celtic Document Supplies, which mitigated closure costs of more than £5 million had a sale not been agreed. All staff retained their jobs, which had been at risk.
- Improved departmental efficiency as a result of conducting work-flow assessment which highlighted log-jams. Reorganised staff roles to move to new more streamlined work processes.
- Facilitated greater liaison between finance and front-line managers by arranging for finance staff to each spend some time in different areas of the business to increase understanding and enhance relationships. This led to managers involving Finance at an earlier stage in the budget-setting process which subsequently improved the quality of the information being received.

Head of Management Accounts • Clarkson Toys • 1990–1995

Managing team of two for this international manufacturing company with turnover of £50 million.

- Spotted discrepancies in financial information which uncovered fraudulent practices in a geographically remote part of the business.
- Developed new way of presenting financial information for non-financial managers that helped them to understand more easily the financial performance of their department.
- Trained and developed three new members of the Finance Department in the new financial management software.

Corporate Cost Analyst • W and H Atkins Limited • 1988–1990

- Produced complex costing reports for senior management presentations.
- Advised department heads on financial performance against targets with recommendations where required.

Education and qualifications

Member of CIMA since 1990

BA Business Studies (2:I) University of Colchestershire

J Chapman 2/2

CVs for internal promotions

If you are applying for an internal post, perhaps a promotion, you need to undertake the same degree of research, preparation and hard business sell that you would use for an external vacancy.

- Fully research the role. Do not make assumptions as to what you think the role is. You simply have no excuse for ignorance. Go speak to the manager, HR, other people who have key relationships with the post-holder to find out what the ideal candidate will offer.
- Do not assume that the interview panel, even if it is your current manager, will know everything about you and your achievements. Spell these out on your CV. They need reminding of your good points.
- Emphasise that you are an easy person to hire as you know the organisation so can 'hit the ground running'. This gives you an advantage over an external hire.
- If you are in competition with another internal candidate never criticise or try to undermine them either subtly or overtly. Focus on the positives that you have to offer.
- Your CV will need to be truthful as it will be examined by people who can contest any claims you make that are unsubstantiated. Be careful as to what you claim as your achievements or abilities – just make sure that you provide plenty of examples to prove them.
- The most common fault of candidates applying for internal promotions is modesty. They assume their current performance will be enough to convince the shortlisting panel. It won't be. Be confident, realistic and show your enthusiasm and capabilities for the new role.

Using the format guidelines from Part 3 and the content you have collated from Parts 1 and 2, it is now time to sit and write your version of your CV. Use the checklist in Table 12 to help you.

TABLE 12: CHECKLIST FOR YOUR CV

Contact details are complete and fully functioning	☐
Career profile/objective matches target role	☐
All factual information is accurate	☐
Positive action words used throughout	☐
Gives examples of achievements	☐
Gives examples of key skills in action	☐
All relevant qualifications including training are included	☐
Gives examples which show your positive personal qualities	☐
Presentation of CV is smart and professional	☐
No more than two pages	☐
Format of CV is checked for compatibility with recipient software	☐
Spelling and grammar is perfect	☐
CV is always accompanied by covering letter/email	☐
Feedback obtained from at least three people to check that it is error free and conveys desired impression	☐

IN A NUTSHELL

This chapter has looked at some situations where CV content and layout requires slightly different treatment in order to help you present as a strong candidate. However, always remember that the same three rules will apply regardless of your particular CV challenge:

- tailor the content to provide examples that you have exactly what the employer is looking for
- use a format that right on the first page enables you to prove you are the ideal candidate
- pay attention to the professional layout of the CV, which will be taken as an indication of your approach to your work.

HOW TO USE YOUR CV

How to use your CV

Part 3 showed you how to write your CV. Now you need to know what to do with it.

The whole purpose of the CV is to get you interviews, so Part 4 of this book is designed to help you with the etiquette of applying to organisations and the different job-search strategies available to help you obtain a meeting with your target employer.

14 SENDING YOUR CV BY EMAIL OR POST

You have spent considerable time and effort in researching and writing your CV. However, even with a great CV you can inadvertently sabotage your chances if you don't pay sufficient attention to the way in which you send your CV to the employer.

This chapter will help you:

- understand the dos and don'ts of email correspondence and sending a CV by post.

- ensure your CV is readable by the recruiter.

- write a covering email to accompany your attached CV.

The growth in technology has meant that few of us send letters by post any more. In business as well as in our personal lives, we now tend to use email. When applying for a role, you are most likely to correspond with a prospective employer by email and to send your CV usually as an attachment to an email address which may be the HR department, a named individual or an agency.

The frequency and immediacy with which we send emails means that it can be easy to underestimate or misjudge the impact that an email can make at the other end. While on an everyday basis we may use email informally, when you are applying for a job, great care should be taken with all communication with an employer.

Format compatibility

Your first step is to double-check the format in which you are sending your CV to ensure it is compatible with the recipient's software. Recruitment websites will usually give guidance about the file size and/or the format. You are usually fine if you are using standard fonts and layouts in Microsoft Word, e.g. Arial, standard margins.

However, if you are using a more unusual font, graphics, widened margins, columns, boxes or even underlining and italics, then there is a risk that the version you send will look very different when the recipient opens your CV their end. The spacing will often slip which will make it look very odd. Photos, graphics or logos in your CV may also be blocked by vigilant virus and spam filters.

If you want to send a feature-heavy CV, you may want to save it in PDF format, which will preserve the layout. However, you will need to check that your CV can be uploaded in this format for a recruitment website.

If in any doubt, the safest option is to create a CV in plain text format. This is more limited in its features but the advantage is that its format is easily read by other programmes.

The easiest way to do this is to open your nice new CV in whichever programme you have created it in and then in the save options, click to save it as a plain text document (*txt). You will then see that the format changes. You will have fairly limited options in terms of presentation, but if you make it look good within this document and then save it, you will have a CV that you can send anywhere and the recipient will see your document exactly as you do.

Email etiquette

- Remember that applying for a job is a formal process and your manners should be formal. 'Hiya' or equivalent is not the way to address your email. Use the individual's name if known, 'Dear Jane' or 'Dear Jane Brown'. If you do not have their name, use 'Dear Sir/Madam' or 'Dear Recruitment Manager' or equivalent. If you write 'Dear Sir' when you do not know who will be opening your email, then you run the risk of offending any female who receives your email and vice versa.

- In your covering email, write in full sentences, but use bullet points to emphasise any key points.

- Never use text-speak as you would on your mobile.

- End the message formally, e.g. 'I look forward to hearing from you' rather than a 'Thx!' type ending.

- Always check and double-check the spelling in the main body of your email and any attachments. Spelling mistakes mean landing on the reject pile 99.9% of the time. Remember the spell-checker won't pick up every spelling or grammatical error.

- When sending your CV as an attachment, always label the attachment with your full name and reference number or date to keep track of the version you have sent. Also indicate which job you are applying for, e.g. msmith604mktgmgr.doc. This ensures that your CV will be easily identified.

- Don't use your work email address. Set up a private email address specifically for job-hunting. You can obtain free email addresses from Hotmail, Google and Yahoo among others.

- Be aware that employers are likely to monitor the email and internet use of their employees on their work computers so if you use work facilities or work time to apply for jobs then be prepared to explain why to your boss.

- Exercise caution in sending out your personal details. Is this a company that you know or who you can verify independently? If you are unsure, take a look on the web and see if you can find out anything about the company before sending out your confidential information. Identity fraud is sadly commonplace now and the information on your CV, your contact details, occupation, etc. could be of high value to someone who wanted to pretend to be someone else.

> Title your CV as though you were explaining yourself in one line! The first thing employers see when they search CVs is the CV title. A title such as 'CV 1' isn't going to mean too much, nor will it help the employer find you in their search. Give your CV a rich title such as 'Product Manager with HTML, JavaScript and project management experience'.
>
> *Michelle Brown*
> *Head of*
> *Communications, Monster*

Writing a covering email to accompany your CV

If your CV is attached to the email, then use the main body of the email as your covering letter. Tell the employer how you meet their key requirements so that you can immediately make a good impression and entice them to open the attachment and look at your CV in more detail.

- In the subject line of the email, list the vacancy title, reference number and where you saw or heard about the vacancy.
- Use the body of the email to convince the recruiter in three to five bullet points that you are the right person for the job.
- Send the CV as an attachment clearly labelled with your name.
- Spell-check before sending the email.

EMAIL COVERING LETTER

To: Ann Brown
Subject: Project Manager, ETD, Ref No. 1234 Management Today
Attachment: MwoodCVfeb08.doc

Dear Ann

I am interested in applying for the above job as I believe my substantial experience in project management combined with my knowledge of the telecommunications sector will be of particular benefit to your organisation.

ABC has an excellent reputation for innovation and having worked on a number of ground-breaking technological projects from the planning to the implementation stage, I believe that I can make a significant contribution to your organisation.

In particular, I have:

- 10 years' experience in managing teams of between 5 and 15 people on a variety of complex telecommunications projects

- An engineering background which gives me the ability to quickly grasp new technical detail and assess implications for operational planning

- Experience and qualifications in PRINCE2 project management software

- Superb relationship-building skills enabling project team members to focus on task even during challenging times.

My CV is attached, providing further information on how my career background meets your requirements. I would welcome the opportunity to meet with you in person to discuss this further.

I look forward to hearing from you.

Mike Wood
Tel: 07777 555 555

CHECKLIST FOR EMAILING CVs

The following is a quick checklist for use before sending off those emails.

TABLE 13: CHECKLIST FOR EMAILING CVs

	Tick when checked
Your CV attachment if sending in Microsoft Word:	
• Arial or Times New Roman size 10–12 for body of text and size 14 for headings	☐
• Standard margin lengths	☐
• Bold used sparingly, principally for headings	☐
• No columns, boxes, underlining or italics	☐
• No graphics, photos or Jpegs	☐
• No shading	☐
CV attachment if sending as PDF:	
• Checked that recipient/website can upload or view these	☐
CV attachment sending from or to a Mac:	
• Double-check format to ensure CV is compatible with recipient's software	☐
Has all the spelling and grammar in the email covering letter been double-checked?	☐
Have you specified in the Subject Line of email the vacancy/reference number of the job for which you are applying?	☐
Does the email covering letter state why you are a good candidate?	☐
Is the covering letter written formally, using full sentences with bullet points to reinforce key selling points?	☐
Have you addressed the individual by name, if known, in the covering letter?	☐
Have you labelled your CV attachment with your name?	☐
Have you created an email address just for job-searching?	☐
Have you included your telephone number in the main body of your email to make it easy for people to contact you?	☐

Sending CVs by post

This is much less common than it used to be. However, there are some good reasons why you may want to send a CV by post:

- You haven't been able to discover the email address for the individual whom you want to send your CV to. This is particularly common if you are making a speculative approach to a company and they won't release the email of the manager you are interested in working for. In this case, you can send it in the post addressed to them personally.
- You seem to be getting lost in the employer's online database and therefore want to send it directly to the manager responsible for hiring staff.
- You are a creative expert and want to send a more visually interesting CV and/or examples of your work, for maximum impact.
- You want to speculatively approach an organisation, perhaps a smaller or more traditional company, where mailing your CV would be viewed more favourably than contacting them by email.

Nowadays, it is relatively rare to send a CV by post rather than by email so it could raise questions about how IT confident you are. Make sure that your CV is of a high standard in terms of layout and presentation and you have a functioning email address on your letter so that they can easily contact you.

I worked for a company operating nightclubs and a candidate sent in his CV in the form of a bottle of Budweiser. He replaced the label with a tiny version of his CV – the bottle was still full – and then sent it through the post to us. It definitely caught the eye and the imagination but he still wasn't successful in his application.

Helen Isaac
HR Manager

On the other hand, the fact that it is now relatively rare, means that it can reinforce your motivation to work for that particular organisation because you were willing to go to the extra time and trouble to post it. And there is no doubt that, compared with an email, posting CVs is more work. They need to be printed off, address written on the envelope, correct postage applied, etc.

SUMMARY CHECKLIST FOR POSTING CVs

- **Covering letter:** always include a covering letter with your full address and contact details. Indicate why you are writing to them and what you can offer that will be of interest to them.

- **Paper:** print your CV on good quality, white or cream paper which has some weight to it. Dark coloured paper should be avoided as it does not photocopy well. If applying for creative/media/graphic type roles you can try a light-coloured paper to make your CV stand out.

- **Print quality::** ensure your CV is laser-printed so the type is sharp and clean. Borrow someone else's printer if necessary.

- **Single sides:** only ever print on one side of paper. Double-sided CVs look messy and the reverse side may get missed when photocopied.

- **Fixings:** do not bind or staple your CV as these make photocopying awkward.

Attach with paper clip, making sure each footer of your CV has your name and page number on it, in case they become separated.

- **Envelope:** put in an A4 envelope rather than folding the CV in half. Too small an envelope will mean that it arrives creased. Ensure that you spell the name of the person, their address and the name of the organisation correctly, and put the right postage on the envelope. Check and double-check these.

- **Gimmicks:** for certain highly competitive creative or media roles, it can be fun to try a gimmick CV. Your CV written on a T-shirt or wrapped around a chocolate bar with a witty message can certainly get you noticed. However, remember that once you have their attention, you still need to demonstrate why they should employ you, so make sure your CV is readable and sells you.

Scannable CVs

Scanning was one of the first innovations in recruitment technology. It involved using a scanner to capture the image of a paper CV and then extracting the key information from the image and saving it on a computer database. The recruiter could then use a report function to search the database using keywords to bring up a report of candidates matching the search criteria.

This software has now largely been replaced by more sophisticated recruitment solutions which can use email or online applications to absorb the required candidate information. However, where companies are still using scanners, they should advise you of this because the OCR (optical character recognition) software has certain limitations on what it can and cannot read. If your CV is going to be scanned, follow these guidelines:

■ send a white, clean, A4 size CV.
■ do not put curriculum vitae at the top – the software will read whatever is on the first line, as your name.
■ choose popular fonts, e.g. Arial, which the software will recognise.
■ use font size between 10 and 14 and make sure the type is crisply printed.
■ use bold only for headings, do not use italics, underlining, graphics.
■ leave out decorative lines, columns, shading or complicated layout.
■ do not staple, fold or fax your CV.

IN A NUTSHELL

This chapter has provided checklists to ensure that when you send your CV either by email or by post, that you continue to reinforce the image of you as a highly professional and capable candidate. Remember that:

■ any communication with an employer is formal and needs great care and attention
■ you need to ensure that your CV will be viewed by the recipient in the same way that you have sent it
■ if sending by post, then ensure the CV and covering letter physically look good.

15 JOB-SEARCH STRATEGIES

You are now ready to use your CV. So where is your ideal job? This chapter is going to look at how you can find it and how you can use your CV to start opening the doors to the interview room.

This chapter will help you:

- tackle the advertised job market

- learn about speculative approaches to uncover the unadvertised jobs

- understand what recruitment agencies and headhunters want from your CV.

L et's look at the main job search strategies in turn and how you can use your CV to good effect.

Advertised jobs

The advantage of replying to jobs advertised by an employer is quite simply that you know there is a vacancy available and there are usually some job details so you can assess your suitability beforehand. The disadvantage is that these adverts are so visible that there is high competition from other potential candidates.

You can find advertisements in local and national newspapers, journals, noticeboards, employer websites, etc. Professional, executive and senior vacancies tend to appear in national papers, e.g. *The Sunday Times*, the *Telegraph* or specialist journals. Most newspapers and journals also have online versions with recruitment listings so you don't have to buy the paper to access the jobs section. Here are just a few examples:

- Accountancy Age: www.accountancyage.com
- Broadcast: www.broadcastnow.co.uk
- Campaign: www.brandrepublic.com
- Computing: www.computing.co.uk; www.computerweekly.com
- Design week: www.design-week.co.uk
- *The Economist*: www.economist.com
- *Engineer*: www.engineeringnet.co.uk
- *Financial Times*: www.ft.com/jobsclassified; www.exec-appointments.com
- *Guardian*: www.jobs.guardian.co.uk
- *Grocer*: www.grocerjobs.co.uk
- *Marketing Week*: www.marketingweek.co.uk
- *Media Week*: www.mediaweek.co.uk
- new media age: www.newmediazero.com
- *New Scientist*: www.newscientistjobs.com
- *People Management*: www.peoplemanagement.co.uk
- *Personnel Today*: www.personneltoday.com
- *PR week*: www.prweek.com
- *Stage*: www.thestage.co.uk
- *Telegraph*: www.jobs.telegraph.co.uk
- *The Times*: www.timesonline.co.uk

If you are looking for a job locally, then it is worth checking the recruitment section of the local papers, usually near the back of the paper. Check out local noticeboards at libraries, supermarkets, community centres, as these often include vacancy bulletins as well as local jobs advertised by small businesses.

UK Jobcentres also have a jobs information service that you can access via its website or telephone line. See Chapter 19 for more information.

Most advertisements will ask you to send in your CV. However, if they ask you to complete an application form or give any other instruction regarding the recruitment process, be sure to follow their directions exactly. If you don't, then they will rightly assume that you can't follow instructions and you will not be shortlisted. Whether you email your CV or send it in the post, always remember to add a covering letter outlining your suitability for the post.

The unadvertised market: networking and speculative approaches

You may have heard people talk about the advertised and unadvertised job market. Statistics vary, but it is estimated that perhaps 80% of jobs are never advertised or if they are, the successful candidate has heard about the role in a way other than reading the advertisement. Interestingly, these statistics apply regardless of the type of role sought, so it is as relevant whether you are a first time job-seeker or a CFO.

Other people are a major source of information about prospective jobs and employers. No-one will give you a job just because they know you, but they will tell you about potential opportunities or people you could contact. Be clear about the kind of role/organisation you are looking for and ask **anyone and everyone** you know if they have got any advice for you or ideas on who you should contact. **This is a highly successful method of job search!** Remember to keep your contacts up-dated on your progress and feed back to them if they have put you in touch with someone they know.

Your networking contacts will be helpful if you want to make a speculative approach to an organisation. This is where you use your initiative to proactively contact employers who you think might benefit from your skills. Your networking contacts may be able to arrange an introduction or the name of the relevant manager to contact. You can also scan newspapers and journals for articles on company expansions, new contracts won or problem areas. If you think your skills could be of particular benefit to an organisation, then approach them directly and tell them why.

A covering letter or email is important, and it should emphasise the value you can bring to their organisation. Your CV can be attached, providing more information but if you are approaching them about a role that is different from your career history to date, then it may be better to send a one-page CV (see Chapter 10) or write a more detailed, covering letter outlining what you can do for them and not send a CV until they ask for it.

This proactive approach can be highly successful if you send your CV to a named individual within a company who is in a position to hire you, i.e. the relevant manager. They will know what their immediate and anticipated recruitment needs are and precisely the skills they will be looking for. Don't send it to the human resources (HR) department, which will just refer you to its advertised jobs.

Do be careful to personalise the email or letter though. Find out the name of the relevant manager, with the correct spelling and their email address. Some companies will not disclose this information and if this is the case, then ask for the general email address and mark it for the attention of the relevant department head so that it can be forwarded to them.

If you are sending emails out in bulk, then make sure that the recipients can't see who else you have sent the email to. If you have lots of different company addresses visible in the 'To:' line of the email, then this is rather going to give the lie to anything you have said in your email about wanting to work for that particular company.

Although mail merge can take a little time to set up as it requires an Excel spreadsheet, a database and a template document, it is well worth learning to use if you intend to send out lots of bulk emails. You may also want to send out emails in small batches to avoid them being classified as spam. If mail merge is not possible, it may be easier to personalise and send each email separately to each employer.

Below is a sample speculative email to accompany a CV as an attachment.

The advantage of this approach is that there are often no other candidates in competition with you and you represent a cheap way for the organisation to recruit, i.e. no agency or advertising costs. Its success depends on the strength of your research, the marketing of your skills – and timing. Your letter or email may just land on the desk at the right time. Always follow up your letters by giving a call; be ready with a clear sales pitch about how you can help.

SPECULATIVE EMAIL

To: Raj Patel
Subject: Opportunity to work together
Attachment: smfeb08prmanager.doc

Dear Raj

I am writing to you because Gladstone Motors' international work with clients in the luxury automotive industry is directly related to my particular skills and experience and therefore may be of interest to you.

As a PR professional with over 10 years' experience working for brands such as Ferrari, Porsche and Lexus, I have acquired substantial knowledge of the automotive sector and a deep customer insight. My key expertise includes:

- enhancing global brand awareness through innovative PR and communication strategies

- project managing complex global marketing campaigns

- organisation of large-scale corporate events, e.g. the prestigious Formula 1 events and high-profile charity balls

- utilising lifestyle channels to market luxury brands and deliver cost-effective solutions.

I am looking for a role where I can use this knowledge and experience to good effect, preferably within an international setting.

It would be good to meet you to discuss this further. My CV is attached for your reference and I will give you a ring next week to hopefully arrange an appointment.

Best wishes

Simon McAllister
Mobile: 07555 555 555

Recruitment agencies

Recruitment agencies are paid by employers to find suitable candidates. An agency may be the sole agency working with the employer or it may be in competition with other agencies. Only the agency whose candidate is selected will usually receive the commission from the employer.

Headhunters are impressed by clarity and conciseness. A CV should be neither too long nor too short. It must communicate as much as possible but must never tire or bore the reader. The CV must show the organisations for whom the individual worked, *what they do or did*, the size of the organisation, the scale of the role(s) held. More detail should be given to more recent employment. Include numbers of employees, turnover and budgets. Achievements should be within the section on the relevant employer rather than positioned in a separate section. Anonymity of employment should be avoided at all costs as should generalities on personal characteristics.

Dr Colin Wall and Áine Hurley
Odgers Ray & Berndtson

Recruitment agencies are therefore often under considerable time pressure. This means that they are interested in having clients whom they can easily place. Your CV needs to be very focused and clear about what you want and why you are suitable. If you are looking for a career change, you may find a recruitment agent less helpful. In a highly competitive market, agencies will understandably prioritise obvious candidates over those who it may take a little more imagination to see in the role. It is worth remembering that agencies are under no obligation to put you forward for any roles. They are not working for you but the employer.

Sometimes agencies will want you to reformat your CV in their own house style. This is fine. However, they should discuss with you if they plan to make any edits to the content. They usually take off your contact details to ensure that employers can't hire you directly and cut them out of their commission. Most agencies also have a recruitment database system where they will store your CV and the information it contains. They will use keyword searches to research the database for candidates who match the requirements of a particular job. See Chapter 16 for more information on keyword searching.

When applying for a job through an agency, there is less opportunity to tailor your CV to a particular employer's requirements simply because you are not always told the employer's details until the last minute. You can supply the agency with a few different CVs tailored to different types of roles. You just need to make sure they send the right CV for the right job.

Headhunters

Headhunters tend to be executive agencies that are tasked by an employer to find senior level candidates. This can include sourcing candidates who may not be currently on the job market. The headhunter will then be proactively approaching individuals by using social networking websites such as LinkedIn, acting on recommendations from people in the industry or conducting research on which organisations are likely to employ people with the skills they are looking for and then contacting them directly.

You can increase the likelihood of you being headhunted by:

- being a good networker: so that people in your industry know you
- having a professional profile on social networking websites such as LinkedIn (see Chapter 18). You may also have your own website or blog
- being visible in your industry. Speaking at conferences, writing articles, media activities, industry working groups, etc. enable your name to get known
- becoming a leader in your field so that your advice is sought by others
- researching which agencies operate in your field and sending them your CV. Cultivate a relationship with a headhunter as it could be quite some time before something suitable surfaces. Make sure that you keep them updated if you move; otherwise your successor may get the call for your dream job, not you.

IN A NUTSHELL

- Follow application instructions exactly as requested for advertised jobs.
- Always include a covering letter or email.
- Send a one-page CV for speculative approaches.
- Make sure you personalise each speculative approach.
- Agencies want candidates who are easy to place. Be clear about what you want and give them a CV that presents you as an obvious candidate for that kind of role.
- Increase your visibility if you want to be headhunted.

16 INTERNET RECRUITMENT SITES

Internet recruitment sites are often the first place that job-hunters look for a new role. Sometimes they are the only place. They are a highly competitive marketplace and successful results will depend on a number of factors.

This chapter will help you:

■ understand how to use commercial internet job-search sites to your advantage

■ use keyword search tactics to increase your chances of selection

■ avoid the pitfalls that claim so many candidates.

The growth in commercial job websites has been phenomenal over the past few years, and they have become a key feature of the recruitment market. In 2008 Monster UK reported that it received a staggering 2.8 million visitors per month with over two million CVs on its website.

In addition to the huge job-boards such as Monster, Totaljobs and Fish4jobs, there are thousands of specialist niche job websites catering to particular industries, sectors or roles. They offer some sophisticated services and can be a useful resource while you're job-hunting. Typically they offer candidates the following services free of charge.

- Posting your CV online for prospective employers to look at.
- Facility to search for particular jobs by typing in the criteria you are looking for, e.g. job title, sector, salary, location.
- An email facility which informs you when particular types of job in which you are interested, are posted on the site.
- Careers advice information, e.g. tips on interviews.
- Other resources, such as salary checkers or information on companies.
- Links to other commercial organisations that may or may not be relevant to your job search e.g. online CV services, book stores, etc.
- Discussion forums.

Employers and agencies make a one-off payment or pay a regular subscription to the recruitment website to:

- post details of jobs and invite suitable candidates to apply
- look through the database and select CVs of the candidates they are interested in.

The ease with which candidates can access thousands of jobs at the click of a return key is very seductive. It can be very easy to get sucked into a black hole of internet job search through one of these job-search portals if you are not careful.

Many people do get jobs from these sites. However, it is not uncommon for candidates to spend hours trawling websites for suitable jobs, only to find that when they apply, their application disappears into the ether and is never heard of again.

> Unless you are seeking employment through a modelling agency, you should not be paying either a prospective employer or an agency any monetary amount for work seeking services Display critical information only. Dates of birth, full postal address, etc. are not necessary for your CV. Key contact information is fine. Remove any details such as emergency contact information. An agency or employer may ask for details such as NI as a way of proving your eligibility to work in the UK. However, unless you are intending to take temporary work with an agency, there is no obligation to supply bank details. If you feel uncomfortable in supplying information, ask why it is needed and how the information will be stored. If in doubt go with your instinct.
>
> *Helen Reynolds*
> *Recruitment and*
> *Employment Confederation*

The problem is, quite simply, that it is so easy for people to upload their CV that the competition for any one job is immense. This means that with so many potential candidates, the chances of you being selected are proportionately lower. Unless you have very specific skills and experience, you are likely to be competing with hundreds, often thousands of other candidates.

The effortlessness of applying for jobs online also makes it easier for people to apply for every and any job, regardless of suitability. The poor recruiter then has to wade through many completely unsuitable applications. This makes the chances of the recruiter finding you even more remote.

Even when the recruitment software is able to do some initial screening by ranking candidates according to key criteria, the recruiter is unlikely to look through all applications if there are a large number. As soon as the recruiter finds between 5 and 10 candidates who look good, they will invite those to interview and select from these. They will only go back and trawl through the rest of the candidates if they don't recruit from the interview.

The electronic nature of the applications means that for a job where there is a large response, you cannot determine whether you are going to be in the first batch of clients on their viewing list or the last, even if you meet all of their criteria.

However, there are certainly things that you can do to shorten the odds.

CV compatibility

As we have seen earlier, you must take care to ensure your CV format can easily be uploaded onto the website's recruitment database. Sites differ in their software capabilities including the size of the file you can upload. There is usually some guidance on the site about what will and won't work.

Keyword search

The growth of online recruitment has led to a massive increase in the volume of applications. In turn, this has led to organisations using specialist software to help sift applications electronically so that initial shortlisting is completed by computer before any application reaches human eyes. This means that you have two audiences to convince, i.e. the software and the human who is ultimately going to invite you to interview and hopefully offer you the job. However, if the software

> Recruitment software offers highly advanced searching of records in seconds, and allows users to polish searches for the right candidate by rapidly searching candidates CVs for choice of keywords and phrases. The speed of searching allows users to search through thousands of CVs and have the best matched handful of CVs ranked in order of suitability in seconds. Candidates can increase their chances of being found by using clear, well-structured formats laid out in a logical manner and avoiding over complicated explanations. Recruiters need a quick and concise overview.
>
> *Stewart Davis*
> *Eclipse Recruitment*
> *Software*

doesn't pick you up as a potential candidate then you are never going to get the chance to impress in person.

Recruiters generate a list of potential candidates by using keywords to search through the candidate databases for suitable people as shown in the screen shot here. This makes the information that you include on the database of paramount importance. The screenshot is taken from the Eclipse recruitment software package and shows that for a software sales role, the key requirements include among others, .Net and C++. The recruiter will search for all candidates who have included .Net, C++ and the other specific criteria on their CV and the search report will generate the details of candidates who match. The most suitable will be at the top and then candidates will appear in descending order of suitability.

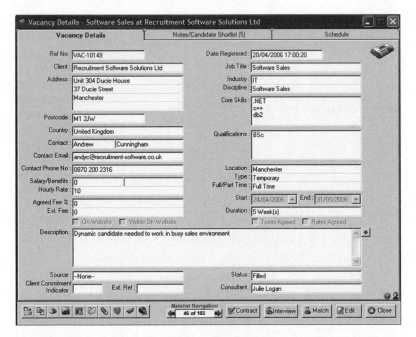

Ideally, you want to weave the relevant keywords throughout your CV supported by lots of practical examples. Some candidates add these as a list in a separate bullet-point section either at the beginning or the end of the CV. However, this has been subject to misuse by some candidates who have indiscriminately included keywords regardless of whether they could be substantiated or not. This has even extended to hiding keyword lists on their CV in white text so that the computer picks them up but the human eye will not.

The difficulty with this is that even if the software generates you as a potential candidate, the recruiter will not be impressed if the detail of your CV bears little relation to their candidate

KEYWORD SELECTION

Use your research from Parts 2 and 3 of this book and the job advertisements and/or person specification forms you obtained for your target role. The skills, experience levels, competencies and qualifications listed there are likely to match many of the keywords that recruiters will use to filter candidates for similar roles. Remember to be specific about your skills, e.g. marketing expertise could include brand management, direct mail, public relations (PR). In addition, if there are particular terms or jargon used in your industry, then include these. However, make sure that your CV is not so overwhelmed by technical terms that the average non-technical recruiter cannot understand your experience.

You may also want to use different terms or names for similar things within the CV, e.g. 'business transformation' and 'change management' as the recruiter may choose one or all of these keywords.

Specify the number of years of experience you have in a certain field as some recruitment software enables recruiters to search for minimum experience by using search criteria such as >4 years' experience in sales management.

List your keywords here:

criteria. In addition, if your CV keeps surfacing for a host of unrelated jobs, then the recruiter may dismiss you as at best, unfocused, and at worst, a time-waster.

Faking it?

Thousands of jobs are advertised on the job website boards but it is sometimes difficult to validate how genuine and current some of those jobs are. Where jobs are posted by an employer you can usually check whether the job is genuine by checking if it is also posted on their corporate website. However, many of the jobs posted on internet recruitment boards are by agencies, so it is doubly difficult to check.

Unfortunately there is anecdotal evidence to suggest that there are agencies out there that advertise non-existent jobs simply to boost their candidate database. A typical scenario is that a great sounding job is advertised with excellent pay and conditions but few specific criteria. This guarantees a large response from a wide pool. Candidates who apply are then told that the vacancy has been filled but their details will be kept on file, even though the advertisement may continue to be posted or reappear at some later date.

Why do some agencies do this? Many work in a first past the post situation so the quicker they can get a suitable candidate in front of an employer the more chance they have of getting their commission if selected. These agencies need a ready stock of good quality, available clients. If their stocks are running low, then advertising a 'dream job' is an ideal way to pull in good-quality clients, even if it is against the Recruitment and Employment Confederation's Code of Practice.

Just be aware that if an advert sounds too good to be true, it probably is.

Publicity shy?

It is important to consider how public you want your CV to be on the commercial job-search websites. Of course, you want all recruiters to be able to see your CV but you may not want your colleagues, competitors or even your boss to see it.

Some sites offer a facility whereby you can block access to your CV from particular organisations. Alternatively you can grant access to the main body of your CV but remove your personal data and contact information. However, bear in mind that you may still be identifiable from your list of employers, educational details, etc. In addition, when recruiters have trawled through hundreds of CVs the question remains, are they going to bother to send you an indirect email via the job site asking whether you are interested, or are they just going to ring up the candidate whose details are more easily accessible?

Making your CV completely confidential means that you can still look for jobs and forward your CV for opportunities that look interesting, but you will miss out on the recruiters browsing through the database looking for suitable candidates. There is a difficult balance to be sought between advertising your skills and retaining privacy and security.

Anyone can pay a fee to a commercial website company to post jobs on the site and/or search through the CVs in the database. The vast majority of people who want to do this are of course employers and recruitment agencies. However, you only need to see the amount of pop-ups and advertisements on many of the jobsites to see that job-seekers are also a target audience for many other companies seeking to market their services.

Most troubling is that there have been instances where job-seekers posting their CVs on websites and social networking sites have been the target of criminal activity. Fake jobs have been used as a means to extract money from candidates and obtain national insurance (NI) numbers, even bank details – it's a gold-mine for anyone wanting to commit identity theft.

Be assured that you should never have to pay anyone for finding you work. This is against UK law and a fundamental principle of the UK Employment Agencies Act. The only exceptions are in the entertainment and modelling sectors where agents represent the 'talent'.

If your CV is going to be public, make sure that you are extra vigilant in checking and re-checking recruiters to ensure they are legitimate. Ensure you have full contact information, telephone, address, website and company registration number before you part with sensitive information.

> Candidates should ensure they don't hold back on including relevant content because of security concerns. Although there have been some incidents of candidate details being stolen these are few and far between and online recruitment sites have rigorous policies in place to protect candidate details.
>
> You can keep your contact and current employment details confidential if you are concerned about this. Then when an employer finds your CV, it's up to you to decide whether you want to let them know who you are. Remember if you upload your Word CV and make your account 'confidential' you'll need to remove the contact details in the Word document!
>
> *Michelle Brown*
> *Head of*
> *Communications, Monster*

IN A NUTSHELL

This chapter has focused on commercial internet recruitment sites and helped you:

- identify the keywords needed to enable your CV to be found by recruiters
- be realistic in your expectations about these sites
- think about how you are going to balance contactability with your privacy and confidentiality.

17 BUILDING AN ONLINE CV

Some recruitment and employer websites will recommend building an online CV rather than uploading your own Word version. There are advantages and disadvantages.

This chapter will help you:

■ understand what online CVs are and how they are used

■ prepare the information you need to include on an online CV.

Building an online CV for a commercial job website

Many commercial job sites provide the option to build an online CV rather than uploading your existing CV. Some employer's websites offer only this option.

If the online recruitment site you are using has ready-made CV templates you can use, this will simplify the process and ensure your CV looks slick and professional when viewed by employers. Having your CV in Word format is more flexible for you, but building your CV online can allow for additional searchable fields being included, so make sure you include all relevant information in your Word CV. Use the review tool when you're done, just to check the final layout.

Michelle Brown
Monster

Online CVs are rather like the traditional application forms. There is a pre-determined format, requesting basic biographical information, career history, qualifications, etc. They also ask some pre-qualifier questions, for example your rights to work in the UK, which need to be confirmed before you can proceed with the application.

The advantage is that you know the information inputted will be in a format which is entirely compatible with the job-site database system, making it easy for it to store and access your information.

The disadvantages are that you have less control over how the information is displayed which will most likely be more akin to a chronological CV with employment dates etc. appearing in reverse order. You may also be asked to complete other information which you would not usually put on your CV, e.g. information about your salary.

When you are inputting the data into an online form, it pays to be as specific as you can. If you are too general, perhaps thinking that you want to leave your options open, recruiters are not going to find you especially when there are thousands of potential candidates for more general roles.

Follow the guidelines in Table 14 to help you increase your visibility on the database to recruiters. Where there is no space limit in the form's fields, list all the information you can. Where there is a limit, prioritise only that which is directly relevant to the type of role you are seeking.

TABLE 14: ADVICE ON BUILDING AN ONLINE CV

Personal information	Make sure all contact details are correct and kept up to date
Education	Specify educational background. Recruiters will look for particular educational qualifications, e.g. BSc Engineering, maths GCSE, so the more you have done, the more likely you are to be found
Professional qualifications	Include all professional qualifications. Leave nothing out. Include professional memberships where appropriate, e.g. CIMA
Training	Remember training and development is not only in the classroom, it can include self-directed learning, reading, attending lectures, personal coaching, etc.
Previous employers	Some recruiters will look for candidates who have worked for particular companies. You will need to specify dates usually in the format the software dictates so make sure these are accurate
Job titles	Use the more common job titles for previous roles and use a mix of titles, e.g. HR officer, Human Resources Advisor, HR Business Partner – increasing the chances of it matching the keyword selection chosen by the recruiter
Location	These forms will often ask your preferred work location. Although you may be flexible, rather than leaving it blank, it is advisable to specify a location. This is because candidates who leave the location open may raise questions in a recruiter's mind about their availability and commitment to work in a particular location. There is usually an option to tick a few different locations if you really are flexible
Salary	The form may ask for your salary requirements. It enables the recruiter to assess your seniority level in your field. Wherever possible indicate a salary range to give you some room for manoeuvre. If in any doubt about salary, then benchmark similar roles on the internet to see the market rate and/or use a salary checker facility, available free on many recruitment websites
Sector	Recruiters will look for specific sector experience. Tick each sector you have worked in, even if they were short-term roles
Keywords	Using the information from Activity 15, sprinkle your keywords throughout your online CV. Sometimes there is also a section for 'additional information' and if you have not been able to insert your keywords within the other database fields, then you can put them in this section

Using keywords to find suitable roles

To save time on searching for roles, there is often an RSS or saved searches facility which enables you to save the criteria for a search and have any new roles fulfilling that criteria delivered to your email inbox or RSS feed reader as soon as new roles are entered on their database.

Michelle Brown from monster has given the following advice: 'To return a better range of jobs, try to think about what employers would be posting their jobs under, for example, search using industry accepted terminology rather than internal variations around an occupation – for example 'Customer Support' trumps 'Member Services'. Look for related Jobs links – you'll be able to get a good idea of what else is connected to the search you are running.

The Monster site uses Boolean logic (find out more at www.internettutorials.net/Boolean.html) which basically means you should use AND, OR and NOT to make your keyword search as specific as you need and also use quote marks to group terms. For example if you want to be a Marketing Manager but don't want PR to be part of your role you should type 'Marketing manager' NOT PR manager. If you want to be a marketing manager or a PR manager you should type 'Marketing OR PR' AND manager.'

IN A NUTSHELL

This chapter has focused on building an online CV

■ An online CV will display your information in an appropriate and easily keyword searchable form.
■ You can cut and paste content from your CV into the fields in the online form.
■ Always remember to include your keywords.
■ Be as specific as possible with all the data.
■ Be selective with your search criteria for jobs or you will be overwhelmed.

18 USING SOCIAL NETWORKING SITES

Social networking sites have become a legitimate place to seek, and be sought for, a new job. They are likely to become an even bigger recruitment forum in the future.

This chapter will help you:

■ understand what these sites are

■ use them as an advertising board to interest recruiters and for networking

■ manage your web presence and your reputation.

Social networking sites

These sites are online web-based social networks where individuals can link with others on the basis of their interests, activities, shared background, beliefs or any other denominator. Some of these networks have millions of registered users while others are more niche. Facebook's own statistics report (www.facebook.com, 2008) that it has a staggering 80 million active users and it is the fourth most trafficked website in the world.

While the under-25s are the heaviest users of websites such as Facebook and MySpace, there has also been a phenomenal rise in professional networking sites, which are more business orientated and aimed at a more mature audience. LinkedIn has become one of the most powerful and widely used of these professional networking sites. In 2008, it had more than 20 million registered users from 150 different industries. There are also industry-specific web forums including networking forums for arts professionals, media workers and scientists among others. Some of these are open to all and others are exclusive, particularly those run by professional bodies such as the Chartered Institute for Personnel and Development (CIPD).

It hasn't taken long for businesses to grasp the huge potential of these sites in advertising to new and niche audiences. They have also realised these communities include people that they may want to hire. These sites are now frequently used by recruiters looking to connect with individuals whose skills are in demand. If you are looking for your next role, these forums have become an important marketplace for you to advertise your skills.

Many of these sites suggest you use one of their online CV builders. This will gather and display information on your career history, qualifications, etc. You can use the information already devised in your CV to copy into the online CV.

Take note that just because these are 'social networking' sites, you shouldn't be misled into taking an informal approach when selling your skills. Do the full sales pitch and pay attention to keywords as this is how recruiters will find you. You can also usually include a link to a personal website page if you have one so that people can find out more about your work and what you do. Most of the sites also ask you to tick whether you are interested in job offers, so make sure this is ticked in your profile settings. Some of the sites also let you add recommendations from other people. This can have a very positive impact if someone is reading your web profile for the first time.

The main purpose of these sites is to network, so do take full advantage of this. Use keywords yourself to try to find individuals who are working in the organisations or roles in which you want to work. You can also contribute articles, advice or opinions on the many forums available on these sites which will help to increase your visibility.

Listed below are some of the key social networking sites. However, this is such a dynamic area that there are bound to be new ones emerging, merging or disappearing all the time.

- Ecademy: www.ecademy.com
- Facebook: www.facebook.com
- Friends Reunited: www.friendsreunited.co.uk
- LinkedIn: www.linkedin.com
- MySpace: www.myspace.com
- Perfspot: www.perfspot.com
- Plaxo: www.plaxo.com
- Twitter: www.twitter.com

(Also see if your professional body or industry area has its own networking forum.)

Your web presence is your reputation

While social networking sites present excellent opportunities for recruitment, it also means that employers, both current and prospective, have become extremely sensitive to their employees' web presence.

Inevitably every professional will have a presence on the web. Therefore it's important for individuals to take control of that presence and make sure that they mould and shape it into an accurate representation of them. Companies are actively using LinkedIn to find people who are the perfect fit for their companies. By maintaining a LinkedIn profile that is up to date and a stellar extension of your professional work, you're putting your best foot forward. You can also display recommendations from past co-workers and clients. That can be a valuable resource if potential clients and partners scour the web for additional details about you and/or your work style.

Krista Canfield
LinkedIn (www.linkedin.com)

The public nature of many of these websites and discussion forums means that any information you have posted under your own name is potentially accessible. Even with privacy controls, it is impossible to guarantee control over who has access to your posted information and who does not.

So, a word of warning! It is very easy for HR professionals or managers to research potential candidates on the internet. They simply put your name in their preferred search engine. Why not try looking yourself up in this way. You may be surprised at what comes up. Some recruiters

The implications of social networking sites for recruitment are quite significant. Look at your social pages from an outsider's point of view. If there are pictures of you falling out of a nightclub door, what image does this give to a potential employer? Many social sites do enable the majority of your content to be viewed only by those contacts you know. So keep your public profile brief but professional. If you want to have an open public profile, don't talk about your job or your employer in a defamatory way.

Fiona Coombe
Recruitment and
Employment Confederation

do this search as a matter of course. They may or may not tell you that they are doing so. You can understand from their perspective that it's desirable and convenient to conduct this check before hiring a new recruit.

Given that social websites such as Facebook are predominantly for social purposes, it is common for people to talk about their personal life. Do you really want an employer to know about your partying habits or to know how you hated working for your last boss? Be careful about photos, as those that portray you half-naked, drunk or pulling funny faces are going to create an impression certainly. However, they are not going to attract many job offers – or at least not the kind you want.

Many organisations have developed staff policies which dictate the kind of information that their employees can submit to these sites and the accessibility to such sites during working hours. This may seem heavy-handed for something that individuals predominantly do during their non-work time. However, when you consider that an individual's criticism of their own organisation could easily surface in a web search by a prospective customer, then you can understand their concern.

Before you post any information in your own name on the web, consider whether you would be happy to have this information published in a national newspaper where your family, friends, current and future employers could see it. If not, then change it. You can never be totally sure who your audience is, so play safe.

IN A NUTSHELL

- Take advantage of social networking sites to advertise your skills and experience and access job offers.
- Use information from your regular CV and cut and paste into the sites' online CV forms.
- Make sure your website presence maintains a business reputation.
- Tick your availability for job offers.
- Actively network on the sites, participate in forums, etc. to increase your visibility.

ADDITIONAL RESOURCES

19 OTHER RESOURCES

This chapter outlines some additional external resources that you may find helpful either in the CV writing process or in meeting your larger job-search or career-management objectives.

This chapter will help you:

- identify the range of free resources that can assist you in devising your CV

- examine some of the commercial career support services available and suggest selection criteria

- provide website listings for other career information resources.

Other people

One of the most challenging aspects of writing a CV is to remain objective about yourself. It can be easy to underplay your skills or 'over-egg' your achievements. So one of the most valuable resources you can utilise is other people.

Try to get a second opinion on your CV from one or more people who know you, whose opinion you trust and who are willing and able to give you honest feedback. Ideally they will know you in a work context and have some knowledge about recruitment and/or your target role. Brief them on the job you are looking for and then ask for their opinion on:

- whether the content makes sense and is relevant
- whether the CV looks good (attractive layout, spelling, etc.)
- what impression they think your CV creates and whether it matches the one you were aiming for

Very often they will be able to flag up areas on your CV that are unclear, or where too much or too little detail is provided. You may get some different, even conflicting views but most importantly you will get some consistent messages regarding what works and what doesn't. This will help you develop a CV that is robust enough to work for all the different recruiters to whom your CV is going to be sent.

Free career support services

In the UK, there are a number of different resources where you can access careers and job-search information for free.

- Learn Direct provides careers information and guidance via its website (http://careersadvice. direct.gov.uk). It offers an online CV builder, skills and values questionnaires, careers software, etc. as well as comprehensive information on all aspects of job searching. It also provides a telephone and email helpline for individuals who have a career, job search or training-related query they wish to discuss. This helpline service is more geared to one-off enquiries rather than ongoing support. Learn Direct is well placed to advise individuals with barriers to employment, e.g. a disability, ex-offenders, those with childcare issues or needing training. This service is free to all adults in England, Wales and Northern Ireland. Its target audience is helping those with few or no skills or qualifications to improve their employability. However, much of the information and resources available via the website are relevant, whatever the type and level of the role being sought.

- Young people aged between 13 and 19 can access careers information and guidance, and welfare support through the Connexions Service at www.connexions-direct.com. Students can usually access a free in-house careers service provided at their university or college. The Prospects website (www.prospects.co.uk) also provides a range of careers resources specifically for students and recent graduates, as well as a selection of low-cost career support services.
- There may be other career support initiatives running in your local area. These may be funded by governmental sources or by voluntary organisations and are often targeted at specific groups such as women-returners or those living in particular geographical locations. You can often hear about these through your local paper or via your local Job Centre.
- Many career-related websites offer free job-searching information and tips on CV writing. Some of the commercial job-search boards such as www.monster.co.uk have excellent information available, answers to frequently asked job-search questions as well as discussion forums where you can seek advice from other job seekers. Some of the largest recruitment sites are:
  - www.monster.co.uk
  - www.jobsite.co.uk
  - www.totaljobs.com
  - www.manpower.com
  - www.topjobs.co.uk
  - www.exec-appointments.com
  - www.fish4.co.uk/iad/jobs
  - www.reed.co.uk
  - www.education-jobs.co.uk
  - www.charityjob.co.uk
  - www.redgoldfish.co.uk
  - www.hays.com

If you are looking to work in a particular sector, it is well worth checking out the website of the relevant professional body or institutions. They frequently offer information on recruitment in their field. Here are the website addresses of some of the key professional associations within the UK:

- Association of Chartered Certified Accountants: www.acca.co.uk
- Association of Young Professionals: www.amicusfoundation.org.uk
- British Computer Society: www.bcs.org.uk
- Call Centre Association: www.cca.org.uk
- Chartered Institute of Building: www.ciob.org.uk

- Chartered Institute of Management Accountants: www.cima.org.uk
- Chartered Institute of Marketing: www.cim.co.uk
- Chartered Institute of Personnel and Development: www.cipd.co.uk
- Chartered Institute of Public Finance and Accounting: www.cipfa.org.uk
- Chartered Institute of Purchasing and Supply: www.cips.org
- Chartered Institute of Taxation: www.tax.org.uk
- Chartered Management Institute: www.inst-mgt.org.uk
- Institute of Directors: www.iod.co.uk
- Institute of Electrical Engineers: www.iie.com
- Institute of Legal Executives: www.ilex.org.uk
- Institute of Leisure and Amenity Management: www.ilam.co.uk
- Institute of Physics: www.iop.org
- Periodicals Training Council: www.ppa.co.uk
- Public Relations Consultants' Association: www.prca.org.uk
- Royal Institution of Chartered Surveyors: www.rics.org.uk
- Telecommunication Managers' Association: www.tma.org.uk
- The College of Law of England and Wales: www.lawcol.org.uk
- The Engineering Council: www.engc.org.uk
- The Royal Society of Chemistry: www.chemistry.rsc.org
- Women's National Commission: www.thewnc.org.uk

There are also sector- or organisation-specific websites that can help, e.g. www.nhscareers.nhs.uk, which provides a telephone helpline for anyone interested in working with the NHS whether they are looking for a clinical or non-clinical role. For those interested in starting a career in the media, www.skillset.org is there to help you. Search on the web to see if there is something similar in the occupational area in which you are interested. Newspapers and trade journals often feature career advice and articles too.

Commercial services

Many of the 'free services' listed above can be extremely helpful. However, because they cater for huge audiences, the advice tends to be generic and the opportunities for meaningful discussions about your particular career situation are limited.

Commercial services on the whole will offer you more individual and customised support, although this too can vary. Listed below are some of the more popular paid-for career services.

CV writing services

Several companies advertise on the internet and in the *Yellow Pages* offering to write your CV for you for a fee. There are also individuals offering their services privately. Prices can range from as little as £50 to over £1000 but the quality and service is variable and not always commensurate with the price.

How it typically works is that you will send a copy of your old CV and/or complete a questionnaire. There may also be a telephone conversation with the person who will be writing your CV. The finished CV is then emailed to you or copied onto a disk along with some hard copies, and sent in the post.

The advantages of using this type of service is that the CV is usually attractively presented and they are produced pretty quickly, often within a week. The disadvantage is that the limited amount of discussion the individual has with the CV writer means that there is often a formulaic approach to writing the CV with an over-reliance on stock phrases. You can end up with a CV that doesn't sound like you at all and which may appear insincere and insubstantial to the recruiter who has read these stock phrases on umpteen occasions. In addition, if you are at all unsure or unfocused about your next role, then this hesitancy is still likely to show up in your CV regardless of who wrote it. If you are thinking of making a career change, then your CV is likely to require a lot more thought and discussion than a CV writing service may be able to offer and deliver.

When considering this service, it is perhaps most important to be realistic in your expectations to avoid disappointment. While there is no guarantee that the more expensive CV writing services are better than the cheapest, it is unrealistic to expect a CV for which you have paid less than £100 to have hours of input lavished on it. You can reasonably expect some prettying up of the presentation but not a lot else. Some companies will be honest with you about this, others more vague.

If your main aim is the attractive presentation of the content then you could also check whether a local secretarial service can provide a more cost-effective solution. However, make sure they are clear about the formatting guidelines regarding CVs.

If you are considering a CV writing service, here are some guidelines to help you choose.

- Choose companies whose websites are well written, clear, functional and aesthetically pleasing. A poorly presented website does not give confidence that your CV will be as professionally produced as required. (NB There are CV writing websites with prominent spelling mistakes on their home page!)

- Be clear on the brief you are giving your CV writer. Highlight the key points you want to emphasise and provide the detail they require.
- Aim for companies that include consultation time between you and the CV writer either by telephone or email.
- Try to find out how much time is allocated for the CV writer to spend on physically writing your CV so you can gauge what degree of input and thought is likely to go into its production.
- Check out the credentials of the person writing your CV and what qualifies them to do this work.
- Ensure you are clear on all costs and what is included for the price.
- Confirm the response time. Some guarantee a completed CV within a certain time. Be clear about the timescale expectation.

Career coach

A career coach is typically someone who will work with you on a one-to-one basis to help support you in creating the working life you want. This may be in the form of face-to-face meetings or telephone coaching. The coaching element means that this service is more personal and therefore better able to take into account the individual's specific needs.

There are career-management companies who specialise in working with individuals to help them make informed career decisions and support them in finding their next role. This can be particularly helpful if you are feeling stuck in your career, want to explore your options and would benefit from support in the job-search process.

There are also outplacement companies who focus primarily on providing job-searching support to individuals who have been made redundant. Many of these will work only with individuals if their organisation is paying for their support. However, some will also work with private individuals who are funding themselves.

You may also be able to find a freelance career coach who will offer career-related coaching options according to their particular expertise.

The advantage of using a career coach is that they can advise you on the more practical aspects of job-searching while working with you on some of the more personal stuff like presenting a confident image, achieving a work/life balance or working out what you really want to do. They are particularly helpful if you are experiencing a career block and are uncertain or unfocused on what next.

The disadvantage is that they usually require a larger investment in terms of finances, time and energy. However, they can represent good value for money if they help you into a role you want, more easily or quickly than you would otherwise have done.

If you decide that a career coach is what you need, then choosing the right coach/coaching company is important. These are some guidelines of what to look for:

- specialist training in career coaching, career guidance or other career-related qualification
- substantial experience of working with individuals in career transition
- membership of an appropriate professional body following a code of practice
- evidence of continuous updating of their knowledge, including the coach receiving regular supervision with a trained coaching supervisor
- expectations are clear, open and transparent and there is a written contract which reflects this understanding and outlines all fees, obligations, etc
- the coaching arrangements are clear regarding meeting venues, telephone arrangements, allocation of time, etc
- you feel comfortable and safe working with the company and coach – trust your instincts on this one.

The Chartered Institute of Personnel and Development has a code of practice for career management and outplacement consultants, and offers good advice on selecting a career coach (www.cipd.co.uk).

Other paid services

You can purchase software to help you write your CV. This interactive software can be helpful in organising your information and often includes an easy mail-merge and record system for applications. However in itself, it doesn't offer much that can't already be achieved easily with Microsoft Office. Although many of these software programs are reasonably priced, there are also free versions available on the web that are being given away by companies trying to attract the job-seeking audience.

IN A NUTSHELL

- Other people are a fantastic resource: ask them for advice, feedback and support.
- Check out the free career information services available to help you.
- Commercial career services can be a good investment: but choose wisely.

20 AND FINALLY...

As you have been reading this book, completing the activities and devising your CV, you have also been acquiring some of the essential skills of career management, that is:

- knowing what you have to offer an employer
- understanding how to research and target the role you want
- the ability to articulate the above to an employer and show them how you can meet their needs.

This means that when you go to an interview and they ask 'Why should we employ you?' you will genuinely know why.

It will also be of immense help to you when you are networking for your next role, looking for promotion or planning a future career change; in fact throughout your career.

The truth is, in a competitive recruitment marketplace, it is not always those who are most capable who get the job – it is those who understand and apply those principles of career management. You are on your way!

Wishing you success!

Corinne Mills
www.personalcareermanagement.com